Congr

You have just purchased
and Feng Shui person

You've made a great investment in your future and you'll love the specialized insights on what to expect in terms of love, business, wealth and career in 2010!

But wait! Don't' Stop Here… There's More!

Now you can discover other powerful feng shui secrets from Lillian Too that go hand-in-hand with the valuable information you will find in this book.

And it's ABSOLUTELY FREE!

**LILLIAN TOO's
NEW Online Weekly Ezine FREE!**

You've taken the first step by purchasing this book. Now expand your wealth, luck and knowledge and sign up immediately! Just go to www.lilliantoomandalaezine.com and register today!

It's EASY! It's FREE! It's FRESH & NEW!

Don't Miss Out! Be one of the first to register at www.lilliantoomandalaezine.com

Lillian's NEW Online FREE Weekly Ezine is only available to those who register online at www.lilliantoomandalaezine.com

LILLIAN TOO & JENNIFER TOO

FORTUNE & FENG SHUI

Sheep
2010

Fortune & Feng Shui 2010 SHEEP
by Lillian Too and Jennifer Too
© 2010 Konsep Lagenda Sdn Bhd

Text © 2010 Lillian Too and Jennifer Too
Design and illustrations © Konsep Lagenda Sdn Bhd

The moral right of the authors to be identified as authors of this book has been asserted.

Published by KONSEP LAGENDA SDN BHD (223 855)
No 11A, Lorong Taman Pantai 7, Pantai Hills
59100 Kuala Lumpur, Malaysia

For more Konsep books, go to www.konsepbooks.com
or www.lillian-too.com
To report errors, please send a note to errors@konsepbooks.com
For general feedback, email feedback@konsepbooks.com

Notice of Rights
All rights reserved. No part of this publication may be reproduced, stored in a retrieval system or transmitted in any form, or by any means, electronic, mechanical, photocopying, recording, or otherwise, without the prior written permission of the publisher.
For information on getting permission for reprints and excerpts, contact: permissions@konsepbooks.com

Notice of Liability
The information in this book is distributed on an "As Is" basis, without warranty. While every precaution has been taken in the preparation of the book, neither the author nor Konsep Lagenda shall have any liability to any person or entity with respect to any loss or damage caused or alleged to be caused directly or indirectly by the instructions contained in this book.

ISBN 978-967-329--033-8
Published in Malaysia, July 2009

for more on all the recommended
feng shui cures, remedies & enhancers for

2010

please log on to

www.wofs.com/2010

and

www.fsmegamall.com

YEARS OF THE SHEEP

Birth Year	Western Calendar Dates	Age	Kua Number Males	Kua Number Females
Metal Sheep	17 Feb 1931 – 5 Feb 1932	79	6 West Group	9 East Group
Water Sheep	5 Feb 1943 – 24 Jan 1944	67	3 East Group	3 East Group
Wood Sheep	24 Jan 1955 – 11 Feb 1956	55	9 East Group	6 West Group
Fire Sheep	9 Feb 1967 – 29 Jan 1968	43	6 West Group	9 East Group
Earth Sheep	28 Jan 1979 – 15 Feb 1980	31	3 East Group	3 East Group
Metal Sheep	15 Feb 1991 – 3 Feb 1992	19	9 East Group	6 West Group
Water Sheep	1 Feb 2003 – 21 Jan 2004	7	6 West Group	9 East Group

You are a SHEEP born if your birthday falls between the above dates

Contents

OVERVIEW - TIGER YEAR 2010 — 10

SHEEP'S HOROSCOPE IN 2010

Part 1. Outlook & Luck for the Year — 42

Part 2. Compatibility with Others
- Sheep With Rat – Boring & dreary — 86
- Sheep With Ox – Double negatives repel — 88
- Sheep With Tiger – In 2010, Feeling bored — 90
- Sheep With Rabbit – Need to try harder — 92
- Sheep With Dragon – Distracted & disinterested — 94
- Sheep With Snake – Blowing hot & cold, yin & yang — 96
- Sheep With Horse – Passionately supportive — 98
- Sheep With Sheep – Hard time to stay upbeat — 100
- Sheep With Monkey – Indifference marks this relationship — 102
- Sheep With Rooster – Rubbing each other up the wrong way — 104
- Sheep With Dog – Strengthening each other — 106
- Sheep With Boar – Romance & comfort with your ally — 108

Part 3. Monthly Horoscopes
- February 2010 – Business & profit luck very good — 111
- March 2010 – Danger of accidents and mishaps — 114
- April 2010 – Financial luck brought by influential man — 117
- May 2010 – Gossip and slander bring worries — 120
- June 2010 – Romantic entanglements bring distractions — 123
- July 2010 – Sheep energy weakens this month — 126
- August 2010 – Grave danger of illness — 129
- September 2010 – Obstacles dissolve and luck improves — 132

- October 2010 – Challenges start to mount — 135
- November 2010 – Money luck but others challenge you — 138
- December 2010 – You could get robbed this month — 141
- January 2011 – Luck from heaven — 144

Part 4. Updating your House Feng Shui
- Yearly Feng Shui Afflictions — 150
- Luck of Different Parts of Home — 154
- Activating Good Star Numbers — 156
- Luck Stars of the 24 Mountains — 160
- Illness Star 2 Hits the NE in 2010 — 161
- Ligitation Star 3 Hits the South in 2010 — 165
- Misfortune Star 5 Hits the SW in 2010 — 168
- Robbery Star 7 Strikes the SE in 2010 — 176
- The Tai Sui Resides in the NE in 2010 — 178
- The Three Killings Flies to the North in 2010 — 182
- The Lucky 4 Star Brings Romance & Study Luck to the North — 185
- White Star 1 Brings Triumphant Success to the West — 188
- Celestial Star 6 Creates Windfall Luck in the East in 2010 — 190
- Updating Your Feng Shui — 193

Part 5. Sheep's Personal Feng Shui Luck
- Finetuning Your Personal Directions — 195
- To Activate Success Luck — 200
- To Maintain Good Health — 204
- Becoming a Star at School — 207
- Attracting Romance — 208
- Interacting with the Annual Lo Shu Number 8 — 210
- Safeguarding Sheep's Afflicted Direction in 2010 — 215
- Improving Your Door Feng Shui — 216
- Special Talismans for the Sheep — 221

OVERVIEW - TIGER YEAR 2010

The Golden Tiger Year of 2010 reflects the character of the Tiger – an aggressive, fierce and tough year that is also resilient and with hidden good fortune possibilities.

There are obstacles due to clashing elements and the aggressive nature of the Tiger makes things worse. We face a scenario lacking in good signs; several traditional indicators suggest a challenging year.

For many animal signs, 2010 is a time of tough choices and hard circumstances. For the Sheep person, the Tiger Year brings a weakening of energy so that both your Life Force and your inner chi strength suffers. There is also the *wu wang* (five yellow) to contend with so 2010 is definitely a year to stay very low key, keeping out of sight of the ferocious Tiger and not taking unnecessary risks.

The 19 year old and 79 year old Metal Sheep are the most badly affected, while Sheep in their prime, the 31 year old Earth Sheep and the 43 year old Fire Sheep are able to pull themselves together and enjoy some success luck. However the 67 year old Water Sheep has excellent finance luck.

INTRODUCTION

> Tiger Years bring out the best in many people. Forced to overcome strenuous situations, many will rise to the challenge. Sheep born people will find that the year brings success to those of you who think positive, act decisively and bring strategic inputs into your work despite the year's afflictions. For you, hard work and belief in yourself is what brings great success, and since all Sheep people have weak chi strength in 2010, it is good to remind yourself of this! Use your strong willpower to subdue bad luck.

The Golden Tiger year does not bring smooth sailing to everyone; only those who stay resilient can successfully transform the year's problems into opportunities. It is vital not to get mentally defeated by the year's fierce energy and feng shui afflictions.

The Sheep born must understand that the year's afflictions can be successfully and systematically subdued. Cures and remedies can be correctly applied so misfortunes can be deflected and avoided. This allows beneficial energy to flow through bringing success and easing of tensions.

The coming twelve months from February 4th 2010 to February 4th 2011 will test the most resilient of professionals, and the most positive amongst us.

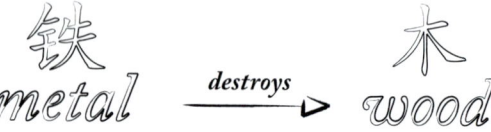

The Year of the Ox just passed has been relatively stable but nevertheless fragile. The Year of the Tiger is less stable, and conditions for work and business will be more difficult.

This is a year when the elements clash directly – the **Metal** of the year's heavenly stem destroys the Tiger's intrinsic **Wood**. Superficially, this is not a good sign. Yet Metal, when used with skill and under special circumstances can transform Wood into something of great value. So even as Metal destroys Wood, it can transform Wood into an object of value. This is the hidden worth which all should strive to capture.

With the elements of the year clashing, hostilities can get uglier, competition nastier and the environment itself more hostile. Heaven and Earth energy are not in sync. It is left to mankind to use our creativity & prowess to rise to the year's challenges and emerge triumphant.

Natural luck is in short supply. But this does not mean we cannot create our own luck! The year's outlook simply manifest the way the elements of the year have arranged themselves – as revealed in the Paht Chee chart, and in the Flying Star feng shui charts of 2010. These charts have proved accurate in past years and are worth analyzing.

Note however that while the elements of the year influence the way luck manifests on a macro level, it is at the micro levels that an individual's luck is determined; and your elements at the micro level can be enhanced or subdued, can be transformed and made better. Here is where understanding astrological indications and feng shui can be so helpful.

There are ways to overcome negative energies caused by a clash of elements brought by missing elements, made worse by visiting "stars" of the 24 mountains or affected by elements that are hidden in the paht chee chart of the year. The "afflictions" we have to confront in the Year of the Tiger, or in any year, can all be remedied.

Remedial Actions

We can create elements that are missing; replenish those that are in short supply; subdue misfortune stars and strongly activate the positive stars that bring good fortune to any home. This is the feng shui aspect of corrective work that can be done to improve the prosperity potential of your home.

The luck of individuals can also be improved by using element astrology and this is laid out in detail in the section on **Annual Element Horoscopes** which explain how the different elements of the Tiger Year affects you based on your animal sign of the Sheep and also the element of your heavenly stem at birth. This year we also offer suggested remedies. You can examine the pluses and minuses of your horoscopes to improve your luck for the year. You can use our suggestions and take steps to minimize whatever horoscope obstacles afflict your sign.

Determine the elements that are missing or weak in your birth horoscope. Note what element requires replenishment; take note of particular afflictions that can cause you the most problems. Then subdue them. Your animal sign scenario and outlook changes from year to year, so it is important to update.

Four Pillars Ruling the Year
Overweight Wood

The year's ruling four pillars chart shows there is an excess of **Wood element,** led by the Tiger whose intrinsic element is Yang Wood. Tiger appears twice,

PAHT CHEE CHART 2010 - YEAR OF THE GOLDEN TIGER

HOUR	DAY	MONTH	YEAR
HEAVENLY STEM 己 YIN EARTH	HEAVENLY STEM 乙 YIN WOOD	HEAVENLY STEM 戊 YANG EARTH	HEAVENLY STEM 庚 YANG METAL
EARTHLY BRANCH 乙卯 RABBIT WOOD	EARTHLY BRANCH 辛酉 ROOSTER METAL	EARTHLY BRANCH 甲寅 TIGER WOOD	EARTHLY BRANCH 甲寅 TIGER WOOD

HIDDEN HEAVENLY STEMS OF THE YEAR

YIN WOOD	YIN METAL	YANG EARTH YANG WOOD YANG FIRE	YANG EARTH YANG WOOD YANG FIRE

The year is desperately short of WATER

in the Year and in the Month Pillars, making its influence and that of the Wood element very strong.

Note also that another Yin Wood is brought by the Rabbit. So there are three **Wood branches** in the chart. These are supplemented by yet another Wood, i.e. the Yin Wood stem of the Day Pillar, making a total appearance of **four Wood elements in the chart.** The intrinsic element of the year is therefore **Strong Yin Wood.**

This excess of the Wood element suggests a year fraught with competitive pressures, when even friends can become devious in the interests of surviving through a tough time. But the Wood element will get depleted.

Two Earth elements symbolically distract Wood, and two Metal elements symbolically destroy Wood. This would have been fine if the Wood was being renewed by the presence of Water. The chart however is missing Water and missing Fire. The Wood of the year thus signifies dead and dying wood that cannot grow. With crucial elements missing, expansion and productivity is greatly strained this year. The work scenario is tough!

Unbalanced Chart

With two elements missing and with too much Wood, the chart is considered unbalanced. This is not an auspicious sign. The presence of both yin and yang pillars makes up for this imbalance to some extent as neither positive yang nor negative yin energies dominate.

Two Metal in the chart suggests that power and rank come into focus during the year. There is no lack of leadership or mentor luck, and there is both yang as well as yin metal, male and female. Powerful men and women play a big role in the year's outlook.

INTRODUCTION

Two Earth elements in the chart signify the presence of wealth luck. There is more wealth luck this year than last year. So despite an imbalance of elements in the chart, prosperity luck is present. This means **there are opportunities for making money** during the year.

> What is needed to actualize wealth luck in 2010 is Water. It is only when the year's Wood element can flourish, grow and bring itself to fruition that money can be made. Wood needs Water, which is missing; WATER must thus be created!

The missing Water is significant. In addition, Fire is also missing. Without Water there can be no growth luck, and without Fire, there is no creativity! In the chart, the Fire element symbolizes ingenuity, intelligence, strategic thinking and mental clarity. Without clear foresight and creativity, the year lacks the spark to get things moving.

Those wishing to succeed must generate the Fire element within their living space, or personify this element by wearing the shades of the Fire element – red. Only then will you be resourceful enough to forge ahead. What is needed in a Tiger Year is vision and imagination. If you can think of original ways of moving ahead in your career, you will benefit greatly.

Hidden Elements

Since the year suffers from missing elements, we next examine if there are any hidden elements in the chart. Usually earthly branches always have hidden heavenly stems and in 2010, the three animals of the year; i.e. the Tiger, Rooster and Rabbit do bring additional elements that supplement the year's luck further. The Tiger hides yang Earth, yang Wood and Yang Fire in the chart, and since Tiger appears twice in the chart, there are **two hidden Yang Fire.**

This suggests hidden creativity, resourcefulness and ingenuity as a result of which the year benefits. This is a good sign. And since Fire exhausts Wood, its hidden presence will also subdue competitive pressures.

However, there is no sign of hidden Water!

This serious lack of water means that although the essence of the year is Strong Wood, missing Water suggests rotting and depleting wood. It is hard to accumulate asset wealth in 2010. Those of you who create a water feature in your work or living space are certain to benefit. Water is what brings excellent feng shui to the year 2010! Note that it is the 67 year old **Water Sheep** enjoys the best of this year's energies in terms of Success and Financial Luck!

Crouching Tiger Hidden Dragon

A significant observation of the 2010 paht chee chart is the presence of the **Rabbit** which belongs to the Wood element, same as the Tiger. The two animals are symbols of Spring, and when combined with the **Dragon,** a trinity of animal signs get created that produce a very strong *Seasonal Combination of Spring*. These three animals rule the East and their combined strength is enormously empowering, especially as their presence is conducive to **creating auspicious new beginnings**!

The Paht Chee Chart of the year contains all the ingredients required to generate the auspicious presence of the Dragon. It is thus extremely auspicious to invite the Dragon image into your home in 2010.

The good news is that the Crouching Tiger can cause the Hidden Dragon to surface. This is the source of the well known descriptive phrase "Hidden Dragon, Crouching Tiger" made so famous some years ago by the Ang Lee directed movie of the same name.

And since the Month Pillar of the year's chart has Yang Earth, this is the ingredient required for the Dragon to rise from the ground and to fly magnificently into the skies. If this energy can be simulated, the Dragon creates the precious auspicious breath that brings good luck. It is thus significant that there is also the presence of Rooster in the chart as the Rooster is the Dragon's secret friend! The Rooster symbolizes the Phoenix enticing the Dragon to make an appearance!

The paht chee chart of the year, possess all the ingredients required to generate the auspicious presence of the Dragon! It is very auspicious to invite the Dragon image into your home.

The Dragon is the celestial creature that will bring great good fortune to the year 2010. So it is really beneficial to place a miniature waterfall which features the images of the crouching Tiger, hidden Dragon and the Rabbit in the East sector of the home.

INTRODUCTION

In 2010, this direction is visited by the celestial heavenly star of 6 which brings good fortune. Placing Water in the East not only activates the luck of a good Spring, it also makes up for the lack of a lap chun caused by the lunar year starting late.

> The key to creating good energy for 2010 is thus a Dragon/Tiger/Rabbit water feature in the East!

The wearing of any kind of precious or semi-precious **earth stone** or of any kind of **Dragon jewellery** is especially meaningful in 2010. The stone signifies Earth which brings wealth luck, while the Dragon activates the luck of new beginnings, transforming the year's Tiger energy to work powerfully in your favor.

Remember that the Dragon can subdue the fierce Tiger and what is needed is the mentally charged energy to activate the chi energy! The presence of the Dragon image completes the seasonal trinity of Dragon/Tiger/Rabbit.

Auspicious & Dangerous Stars

In 2010, two potentially auspicious stars and two potentially dangerous stars make an appearance. Both stars are powerful in their beneficial and malefic influences respectively. The two lucky stars bring good fortune. They impact different animal signs differently and in varying degrees but they are generally beneficial.

1. Mentor Star

In Chinese astrology, much is made of "mentor" luck, which in the old days was an important factor bringing career success. This star might well benefit the 31 year old **Earth Sheep** as well as the 43 year old **Fire Sheep**, despite their weak chi essence. For them, activating for a mentor to bring influence and opportunities will be very helpful for them to actualize their success, which is quite high this year.

The mentor can be a godparent, an elder cousin, a boss or an influential uncle or aunty. Activating the mentor luck in the chart by hanging a picture of your "hero" or someone you respect in your NW corner will energize the mentor into real life! Remember that success often comes from "who you know rather than what you

INTRODUCTION

know." This star is also referred to as the Heavenly Virtue star. With its presence in the chart of the year, it indicates that help comes from powerful people. To activate for this star to manifest successfully for you, use the **Double Six Big Smooth amulet**, an amulet comprising six large coins laid out in a row.

2. Star of Prospects

This favorable star brings a special energy that rewards determination and staying power. Those who have a passion for success will benefit from its presence. There is nothing that cannot be achieved for those prepared to work hard. Here we see ambition playing a big role in making the best of what the year brings. To activate this star in your favor make sure you have a Rabbit image in the water features placed in your home. This advice is especially directed to the 31 year old **Earth Sheep** whose health luck is vigorous. Using Water to activate this Star of Prospects will give strength to your success and finance luck.

The Star of Prospects bring success to those with determination and ambitions. It rewards those who are focused.

3. Star of Aggressive Sword

This star is brought by the Tiger and there being two Tigers, it suggests that the Aggressive Sword's negative effects comes with a double whammy. This star brings fierce, ruthless and violent chi energy. People will push ahead at the expense of others using fair means or foul. The name of this star is *Yang Ren*, which describes yang essence (as in yin or yang) sharp blade that inflicts damage. This star has great potential for good or bad influences to materialize during the year, but it is more negative than positive. The excess Wood in the year's chart makes things worse.

To protect against falling victim to this star's aggressive influence, wear the **Double Ring Talisman**. Also excellent for overcoming the ferocity of the Aggressive Sword Star are the **Trinity Ring** and pendants signifying heaven, earth and mankind chi. These come with powerful mantras of the Lotus family of Buddhas – Amitabha, Chenrezig and Manjushuri.

Wear the Trinity Ring with mantra to protect yourself against the Star of Aggressive Sword. This Trinity Ring also signifies the trinity of *tien ti ren* - which is very auspicious.

Finally, a third remedy is the **Fire Magic Wheel** for those who may be especially badly hit by the year's fierce Tiger energy. If you find yourself falling ill a lot or being hit by big doses of bad luck and disappointments, any one of these amulets are powerful ways to repel the bad luck.

4. Star of External Flower of Romance

This is sometimes confused with the *peach blossom star* because it addresses the destiny of love. When the *flower of romance* is present in any year, it suggests love blossoms easily between people but it is not the kind of love that leads to marriage and family; it indicates instead, the possibility of extramarital affairs bringing stress to happily married couples.

There is a difference between internal romance and external romance, and in the Year of the Tiger, it is the latter rather than the former that prevails. So the year will see increased occurrences of infidelity.

In 2010, the Rabbit in the Hour Pillar is the Romance Star of the Tiger, and because Rabbit occurs in the Hour Pillar, it signifies the *external romance star* and this makes all marriages vulnerable.

Things are made worse by the Rooster in the Day Pillar, as Rooster clashes with Rabbit. This causes misunderstandings, although for the most part, infidelity in 2010 does not lead to divorce.

What all this means for the Sheep is that there could be marriage strains and problems bursting into the open, caused by an outside love interest. It is wise to try and stay aloof from temptations. Your chi strength this year is weak, so it is better not to create risks in your marriage.

Feng Shui Chart of the Year

The destiny luck of the year is also influenced by the year's feng shui chart, which reveals lucky and unlucky sectors of buildings, houses and apartments. The chart comprises a 3 x 3 sector grid of numbers that reveals the luck distribution of the year. 2010's chart is explained in detail in Part 4 of this book.

In addition, the fortune-bringing stars of the 24 mountains also affect the luck of the different sectors of your living space. These stars add important nuances to what is revealed in the annual chart, and their combined influences also affect the luck of each individual animal sign. There are 108 different Fortune Stars, but only a handful fly into each of the 24 mountain directions in any year. These bring auspicious or harmful influences, but vary in strength and type each year. The 24 Mountain Stars affect houses and animal signs equally. Some stars bring good luck, some bring misfortune, while others bring protection. When your sign is negatively afflicted and your vitality gets weakened, you should wear specific protective Taoist charms. When your energy is heightened, the stars help you manifest whatever good fortune comes your way. These are explained in detail for the Sheep in Part 5 of the book.

Monthly Readings for the Whole Year

This book contains month to month readings of your luck to highlight the different chi energy of each month. They reveal significant high and low points of each month. The idea is to be alerted auspicious as well as unlucky months.

For the Sheep born, do note that the Hsia calendar months of Horse (June), Dog (October) and Rabbit (March) will be months when allies and friends make the energies favorable.

Nothing works better than to be prepared for sudden reversals of fortune, and in knowing when a particular misfortune can happen. When forewarned you have enough time to put remedies into place and to wear cures to suppress the affliction. This is the best way of avoiding misfortunes! Better to subdue bad luck than to wait for bad things to happen and then regret.

This is what motivates us to carefully research and analyze the Almanacs and source books to bring you accurate monthly readings that are an essential component of these books. Timely warnings are given in the monthly readings on Career, Business, Family, Love and Study luck.

These take account of each month's Lo Shu numbers, element, trigram and paht chee luck pillars. These are usually very accurate not just in identifying your good and bad months; they also offer valuable advice on when to lie low and when to move bravely and confidently forward. It will help you to get your timing right on important decisions and actions.

Our books on the 12 animal signs this year follow our tradition of bringing advice that is specific, focused and timely. The recommendations here are meant to alert you to months when you are vulnerable to illness, accidents or dangers. The good luck months are when significant opportunities come to you. Knowing *when* is certain to give you a competitive edge. This year we have added new dimensions that bring yet greater depth to our recommendations on timing.

Feng Shui of your Living Space

A section is devoted to vital Feng Shui updates to be attended to at the start of each New Year. This explains transformational energy patterns that create new lucky and unlucky sectors in 2010. You can then make all the necessary adjustments to the feng shui of your home and work place. Remedial cures are always necessary to dissolve bad energy that bring misfortune, accidents, illness and other afflictions. All houses are affected by new energy patterns. You may have enjoyed good feng shui last year, but the pattern of chi will have changed in 2010.

An excellent example is the SW sector of the home, which is the home location of the Sheep. Last year, this sector enjoyed the wonderful Heavenly Star of 6, but in 2010 this year, it is seriously afflicted by the *wu wang* or Five Yellow star, which brings some rather severe misfortune! So luck changes from year to year and sometimes these can be very large changes.

Element therapy is very effective for neutralizing bad energy patterns such as the illness star and for strengthening the good sectors. This year, the **good luck star number 8** is in the center of the chart. This development indicates that the year strongly benefits those whose homes have open plan concept that does not "lock up" this auspicious star number.

If you have a toilet or a store room in the center of the home, this can cause good luck to dissipate or stagnate; but if the center of your home is an open space, the good fortune chi flows seamlessly into the living areas of the home; and then 8 in the center brings extreme good fortune, more so when you install a **bright light** here.

When the luck of 8 of the center is able to flow to other sectors, it particularly benefits the SW and NE, as these are locations visited by the afflictive stars 2 and 5, two Earth numbers that transform into potential good fortune stars when they connect with the 8 to form the **parent string combination of 2/5/8**. Such a configuration which suppresses the negative aspect of 2 and 5 is only possible when there are no walls to block the energy of 8 from flowing outwards.

Generating Wealth Luck in 2010

This is not going to be an easy year for everyone and for the Sheep, the affliction of the *wu wang* makes it worse! This creates the potential for things to go wrong unless the *wu wang* is kept effectively subdued. Once the remedy is in place, then those of the Sheep who have wealth luck in their element charts will be able to create new prosperity for themselves. However, any new wealth created will not be the kind of mega quick bucks generated through escalation of capital appreciation. Instead, wealth will be made in new areas of creative enterprise. It will also be risky because the Year of the Tiger always holds risks. Riding the Tiger requires courage and nerves of steel! Since the Sheep person is rather averse to taking risks, they are advised to go for opportunities that bring safe and steady growth.

The world's economy is presently going through a major transformation; we are living through the Age of an Information Revolution where news/technology and ideas are accessible to everyone. New wealth comes less from traditional sectors and more from new creativity, technology, energy sources and ways of packaging. In short, from inventive product and service initiatives.

> It is advisable to start the Tiger Year by being defensive. You will benefit from being protected so make very sure to place cures in all the afflicted sectors of your office and home. It makes sense to subdue the ferocious side of the Tiger.

For those with dreams of making money and are prepared to take the risks, you can symbolically "ride the Tiger to activate its wealth enhancing potential" but if you are planning on taking business risks this year, then you are well advised to enlist the aid of the "Tiger-subduing deities".

Most famous of the Taoist deities are the **Tiger-Taming Lohan**, the **Wealth God sitting on a Tiger**, and the **Immortal astride the Tiger.** Chinese legends contain tales of the wealth-bringing prowess of wise old Tiger, but this can only be unleashed when the wild side of this ferocious beast is adequately tamed!

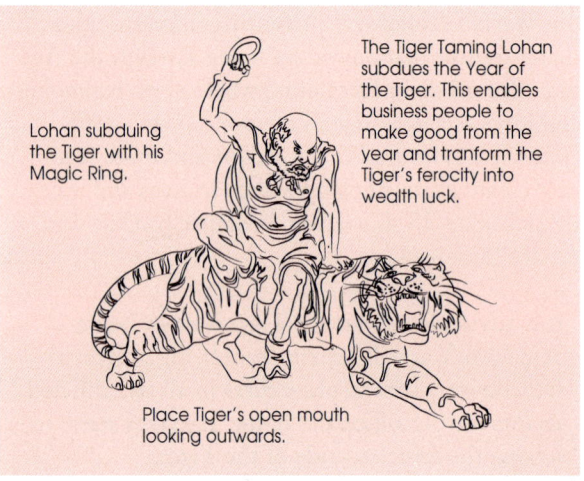

The Tiger Taming Lohan subdues the Year of the Tiger. This enables business people to make good from the year and tranform the Tiger's ferocity into wealth luck.

Lohan subduing the Tiger with his Magic Ring.

Place Tiger's open mouth looking outwards.

INTRODUCTION

Hence in the Year of the Tiger, it benefits to invite in the three powerful deities who are close to the Tiger into your home. To many Chinese, they are the most powerful of Wealth Gods and their presence in any home or office attracts abundance.

You can also energize the Earth element for the center of the house to attract wealth luck and this is because Earth energy stands for wealth luck in 2010. To signify Earth, nothing works better than a circular orb rotating in the center of the home to attract wealth luck.

So a powerful wealth energizer for the home or any living or work area is to have a **solid rotating crystal ball** in the center. Those that come with an 8 embedded in gold in the center of the crystal ball are the best, although those who believe strongly in the power of mantras can also place the *Om Mani Padme Hum* rotating crystal ball here.

Last year we designed just such a crystal ball embossed with the **21 Tara Praises** and these brought so much good fortune for us and everyone who used them. Rotating the crystal ball makes it very yang and that is what makes it generate fabulous energy. Shine a light on the crystal to empower it and to make it even more beautiful.

Horoscope Luck of Elements

Staying lucky requires you to be personally empowered. The aura around you must be radiant and strong, not stagnant and weary. Hence being properly energized, being healthy and staying astrologically strong are the three ingredients of attaining success luck in any year.

What is important is to know exactly how your own personal elements interact with the elements of the year in five important categories. Each of you, depending on your year of birth are born with different elements that affect the strength and quality of your **Life Force**; your **Inner Essence**; your **Success Potential**; the stability of your **Financial Luck** and the state of your **Health Luck**.

Your horoscope reveals the ruling elements that govern each of the five categories of luck, and how they interact with the five luck elements of the year. In 2010, the Life Force of the year is Wood, and its Spirit Essence is Water. Hence you can see that it is Water that strengthens Wood… it is the Spirit Essence that strengthens the Life Force of the year.

The year's Health Luck is governed also by Wood while both the year's financial and success potential are governed by Metal. To find out how each person's birth elements interact with the luck elements of the year, we need to analyze how each person's element interacts with 2010's elements. This provides important information that enables you to enhance your potential enormously.

The analysis is based on your year of birth your heavenly stem and your earthly branch. Once you know how strong or how weak your horoscope elements are in 2010, you can easily dress, live and arrange your living space accordingly. This is discussed in detail for you in Part One of this book.

The Power of Talismans

Protective talismans have the power to ward off misfortunes and each New Year it is incredibly important to know what talismans to wear and place in your home to ward off bad luck. In the Tiger year, its imbalance of energy must be attended to if you want the year to be smooth for you. Protective amulets possess added potency when made correctly. Circular discs and squares are excellent shapes to be used as amulets as these shapes are intrinsically powerful. Built-in Metal element energy of amulets made of steel or brass and with gold finish also have great power to suppress illness and misfortunes.

The Chinese Almanac is an excellent source of talisman designs and good Almanacs provide detailed images with invocations and explanations. These are older, rare editions which we have painstakingly compiled over the years as reference materials to ensure the amulets made comply with vital specifications.

We have discovered that Tibetan-style talismans are very potent; these incorporate Sanskrit and Tibetan mantras which are really extremely powerful. In the old days, Tibetan protection amulets were created by monasteries or very high lamas. These usually comprised mantras and images written onto paper and then folded to resemble mystical knots. Traditional talismans are often covered with 5 colored cloth and tied with 5 colored string, which signify the 5 elements. Modern day amulets maintain the essence of the talismans but their quality of production is much better. In terms of potency they are equally powerful, as modern technology has made it possible to have an incredible number of mantras inserted into the amulets!

Tiger Year Talismans & Rituals

Here are some important amulets and rituals required for the coming year.

The Tai Sui Amulet

This invokes the protection and goodwill of the Tai Sui who this year is once again a military general. This amulet carries a special Taoist invocation with a pair of Pi Yao images. The Sheep is also affected by the Tai Sui, although not directly so it is definitely a good idea to carry the amulet which works by appeasing the Tai Sui. For the Sheep, appeasing the Tai Sui attracts some direct benefits and will help you actualize success luck.

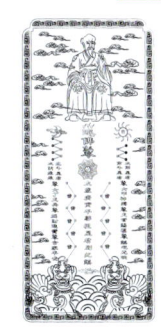

Tai Sui amulet

The Double Circle Amulet

This wards off troublesome chi energy brought by the combination of **Five Yellow** with the **illness star.** Wearing it as a pendant or hanging it in your animal sign direction is an effective way of overcoming troublesome months when the configuration of star numbers bring combined danger of illness and misfortunes.

Double Circle amulet

Good Income Luck Talisman

Fashioned as a wealth vase, this amulet contains the *Taoist wealth fu* written on one side, with coins and ingots on the other side. This talisman is excellent to wear to protect against being laid off, losing one's source of income or to ensure that good business luck continues.

Good Income Luck Talisman.

Blue Water in a Globe

This Water element talisman is a potent way of making up for the lack of water in this year. Carrying this amulet everywhere you go symbolically brings growth luck. Water feeds the Wood energy of the year and this amulet is especially suitable for enhancing good wealth luck. For the Sheep whose natural element is Earth and whose element for success at birth is Fire, generating extra Water element is definitely helpful. Since Water is in such short supply in 2010, literally everyone benefits from energizing for the physical presence of this element.

A drop of water is like an ocean. The Water element brings prosperity in 2010.

5 Element Ringing Bell

The sound of metal hitting against metal creates the chi energy that can dissolve the power of the Five Yellow which in 2010 hurts the matriarch in all families. It is important not only to have this bell displayed in the SW corners of the home, but ringing the bell at least once a week magnifies its strength many times over.

Walk round each of your rooms in an anti-clockwise direction three times, all the while ringing the bell. This is an energy cleansing ritual which is safe and effective to use. It was not easy finding the kind of bells that produce the melodious sounds preferred for these bell amulets. But when you ring the bell you are instantly dissolving bad energy build up in your space. Do this ritual in rooms that are important to you.

Sheep born people should undertake the bell ringing ritual on Thursdays of the week.

5-Element Ringing Bell

The Magic Fire Wheel Talisman

This is the Dharmachakra eight-spoked wheel surrounded by a circle of fire, indicating fire and gold energy. Inscribed in the circle is a very powerful mantra for subduing quarrelsome energy directed towards you. This talisman can effectively reduce gossip, slander, and office politics and even help you avoid court cases and legal entanglements. If you can consecrate these magic fire wheels, they are also effective protection against spirit harm.

Magic Fire Wheel Talisman

The Double 6 Big Smooth Coins

This is a powerful enhancing good luck charm suitable for the year 2010 as it invokes the Star of Powerful Mentors. The six large coins made of metal with gold finish ensure everything goes smoothly for you. Having it in your possession will bring you influential help of someone powerful when you need it. Those in leadership or managerial positions benefit from carrying it.

Precious Ring Talisman

This powerful talisman is said to possess magical powers. It is carried by the **Tiger Taming Arhat** who was a Brahmin named Pindola. Made of steel and plated with real gold, powerful **Dharmakaya mantras** can be inserted inside the ring. It should then be hung in the NE corner of your living room or office, or you can carry it with you as a bag hanging. The precious ring talisman is one of the most powerful ways of subduing the aggressive energy of a Tiger Year.

Hang the Precious Ring Talisman in the NE of your home to subdue the aggressive energies of the Tiger Year.

Part 1
Outlook for the Year 2010

- Metal Sheep – 19 & 79 years
- Water Sheep – 67 years
- Wood Sheep – 55 years
- Fire Sheep – 43 years
- Earth Sheep – 31 years

In this Year of the Tiger, the Sheep is afflicted by the *wu wang*, also known as the Five Yellow and you will have to cope with misfortunes brought by this dreaded affliction. Obstacles that block your progress will manifest and problems stand in the way of your success.

To make matters worse, your chi strength is a double negative this year, as is also your Life Force. This indicates an unfortunate lack of inner confidence and self assurance.

Despite this however, the Sheep is resilient and also blessed with truly exceptional staying power. You possess a certain buoyancy of spirit which, together with your great skill in strategizing, will help you stay on top of the year's challenges.

As a result, Sheep people will enjoy relatively good success in 2010 and some of you – the 67 year old Water Sheep in particular – will even enjoy some unexpected and outstanding financial luck. It appears that in terms of prosperity, this Sheep has it best. The 43 year old Fire Sheep also has good money luck, but that of the other Sheep is average. The 19 year old teenager Sheep has success, but suffers from low levels of confidence and tends to be overly pessimistic.

The luck of the 5 types of Sheep thus vary considerably.

The Sheep Personality in 2010

The Sheep's personality is directly affected by the affliction of the Five Yellow or *wu wang* in 2010. This seriously restricts your options for the year and despite your natural skill at avoiding being directly hit by misfortunes, still the year can be quite hard on you. The biggest consolation is that it all will seem worthwhile towards the end of the year.

Success comes to you... so through the year, anyone dealing with the Sheep cannot help but admire the consistency shown and this despite its show of ambivalence and many times, its indecisiveness. This is all very uncharacteristic of the Sheep personality.

Even for the Sheep itself who is usually strong and vigorous, finding itself lost for words and reluctant to make judgments comes as a surprise. Happily, it all does come together towards the end of the year and early the following year. Much of Sheep's problems come from the arrows of misfortune afflicting the sign, and this is caused by the presence of the number 5 in the chart of the year.

Sheep people will work hard at subduing its impatience at the slow way things develop. You are also put off by the offhand attitude of loved ones, so in your love relationships this year, you could feel hemmed in and stifled. There is a clear feeling of just wanting "out" this year. So if your love life seems unsatisfactory, blame it on the energy level of the year rather than on your spouse. Usually when things appear unbalanced in a relationship the cause is often found within ourselves rather than in others. In other words, causes for feeling dissatisfied come form within and not from external circumstances. This sums up the Sheep's situation in 2010.

Sheep is better off focusing on tangibles rather than on imagined wrongs. It is likely this realisation will make you a lot more subdued as a personality. In any case, you are naturally a mild mannered and non-confrontational sort of person, so staying withdrawn comes quite easily for you.

You know that you have a tough inner core and you know that you do enjoy the luck of success, only that you have to endure setbacks and disappointments. This should help keep you steady. In any case, the Sheep always has friends whose support can be invaluable; and being the 8th sign in the horoscope is particularly lucky in the current period of 8 and with 8 in the centre of the chart this year.

LADY SHEEP

Birth Year	Type of SHEEP Lady	Lo Shu at Birth	Age	Luck Outlook in 2010
1943	Water Sheep Lady	3	67	Fabulous financial luck
1955	Wood Sheep Lady	9	55	Shortage of money luck
1967	Fire Sheep Lady	6	43	Good all round luck this year
1979	Earth Sheep Lady	3	31	In good health through the year
1991	Metal Sheep Girl	9	19	Succeeding at a young age

In 2010, the Sheep lady will seem weak and pliable, projecting an image of fragility and defencelessness that could well melt the hardest of hearts. It is a well known fact that the Sheep lady is extremely subtle in the way she reacts to misfortunes or disappointments, rarely allowing others to see deep into her heart. Outwardly she will be the long-suffering lady attracting both sympathy and goodwill, especially from men who fall for her air of vulnerability.

The Sheep lady always seems to give in to fate, and she will rarely remonstrate against any bad luck that may befall her. So she comes across as a survivor, gamely putting up with setbacks. In any case, Sheep women are rarely the overtly ambitious types and they will never be obvious about their intentions. Having said this, those dealing with her should never make the mistake of underestimating her or even thinking for one moment that Sheep women are weak.

Far from being fragile, Sheep women have the killer instinct, but this is lodged deep inside them. They overpower bad chi with extreme patience and they have their own way of winning through passive non-resistance. So in a year when the Five Yellow could bring enemies, setbacks, misfortunes or betrayals, the Sheep woman will in the end prevail. They will work hard and they will not be obvious about it. But with their patience and subtlety, and almost always helped by their careful practice of the Chinese traditional science of feng shui, in the end they successfully overcome the year's afflictions and emerge triumphant.

The luckiest Sheep lady in 2010 is 67 year old Water Sheep whose money luck is at a noticeable high level.

Perhaps it is her wisdom arising from a lifetime of experiences that helps her or maybe it is her Water element that gives her amazing vitality in a year when most of her siblings are exhausted and feeling weak. Water is very much in short supply in 2010, so that anyone with Water near her or in her birth pillars is sure to benefit this year.

The 55 year old Wood Sheep has extremely low money luck. Its Wood element feels the shortage of Water acutely; this Sheep suffers from the dryness of the year; place some water nearby and things will improve considerably.

The Fire Sheep lady who is 43 years old fares very well indeed during the year, while the 31 year old Earth Sheep enjoys very good health luck.

GENTLEMAN SHEEP

Birth Year	Type of SHEEP Man	Lo Shu at Birth	Age	Luck Outlook in 2010
1943	Water Sheep Man	3	67	Prosperity luck at its height this year
1955	Wood Sheep Man	9	55	Feeling the pinch financially
1967	Fire Sheep Man	6	43	Everything balanced and good
1979	Earth Sheep Man	3	31	Physically very healthy & strong
1991	Metal Sheep Boy	9	19	Success comes despite obstacles

The Sheep gentleman in 2010 is alert and extremely sensitive to whatever changes of energy the year brings. He is instinctively aware of the potential for setbacks and disappointments and is likely to be more than prepared for whatever the year brings. The Sheep gentleman is clever and crafty, always conscious of the unexpected development. So in a Tiger Year, the Sheep will be very much on its toes.

From a feng shui perspective, the Sheep guy should know it is hit by the *wu wang*. And also that he is afflicted and hurt by the double negatives against his Life Force and Chi Strength. This makes the Sheep less enthusiastic than usual. In 2010, the Sheep's usually strong aura is considerably dimmed.

As a result, 2010 will see the Sheep gentleman coming across low key and reticent, more so than usual. He will keep his thoughts to himself along with his insecurities and self doubts, carefully keeping his weakness hidden. In 2010 the Sheep will tend to socialise a lot less, being careful to stay out of the limelight and working more behind the scenes than upfront. In any case, Sheep guys have always been publicity shy; true to the natural characteristics of its sign attributes, he hides his true worth. He will rarely, if ever, allow anyone into his mind.

The Sheep gentleman tends to be uncomfortable when surrounded by too many people. He does not like crowds; in 2010 this characteristic is emphasized so it is unlikely that one will hear much of Sheep guys making the headlines in 2010. Although he is excellent at networking, this is more on a one-on-one basis. He does not work a cocktail party as smoothly as one would expect, but in the safe confines of private homes, the Sheep gentleman comes into his own.

The 67 year old Water Sheep gentlemen are very lucky in 2010 in terms of achieving goals professionally and financially. They will reconcile with loved ones and renew ties with some very old but long standing friends.

Another very lucky Sheep guy is the 43 year old Fire Sheep who also enjoys both success and wealth luck but a lower scale than the water Sheep. Both these high achieving Sheep gentlemen will however need to be careful about any excesses they may have. Health can become an issue soothe advice here is to go easy on the high living lifestyle.

Others of the Sheep sign do not enjoy the same level of good fortune but they enjoy success luck. Challenging and tedious as the year may appear to be, with its disappointments and setbacks, emerging triumphant is nevertheless certain.

Personal Luck Horoscope in 2010

This Section focuses on the Personal Luck Horoscope of the Sheep in 2010 and the chart of horoscopes for each Sheep person is determined by the heavenly stem element of your year of birth.

The Horoscope Chart shows how Sheep's ruling luck Elements in the year birth interacts with the Elements of the year 2010. The Horoscope deals with 5 types of luck with each type being affected differently each year. Each of the Sheep's 5 birth elements interact with those of 2010 and this interaction reveals whether the year brings strength or weakness to that particular type of luck.

It is important to examine what kind of luck combination your animal sign's element horoscope brings you each year. This is because the element signifying the 5 types of luck changes from year to year. The 5 categories of luck and their significance is explained as follows:

First, Your Life Force...

This reveals hidden dangers or threats to your life that can cause premature death or bring severe worries. This can come suddenly, with little warning, and death can also come to perfectly healthy people through accidents or unexpected natural disaster. In recent years raging wild fires, widespread floods, earthquakes and other natural disasters have brought havoc suddenly and unexpectedly into people's lives. So looking out for such threats is an important aspect of horoscope consultations.

When the Life Force luck shows a double cross - XX – as it does this year for all those born in the year of the Sheep, it is vital that the double negative be overcome by wearing a **celestial amulet**. The best form of protection is usually something spiritual, a set of sacred syllables of a talisman that carries powerful holy mantras.

A double XX does not necessarily bring death. What it brings is a warning that some kind of danger is definitely imminent. Usually if the wearing of amulets is accompanied by some good deed such as performing animal liberation or donating to some charity danger is successfully averted.

Threats to the Life Force are usually karmic and these can be assuaged by a specific kind action on your part. Be mindful of your interactive behaviour with others. Guard against arrogance and if you should get into a fight or an argument, do just walk away. Give the victory to those who annoy you!

This may be hard to do, but it is extremely beneficial this year because your Life Force is so weak this year, it is only by being patient and yielding that you can transform any bad luck you may be experiencing this year into good luck.

Second, Your Health Luck...

This is a direct barometer of your physical health and if yours is showing a double cross - XX - it means that 2010 could bring ailments and vulnerability to health issues. When health luck is not good, work schedules and grand plans get blocked.

Poor health luck means you can get food poisoning easily and you can catch wind borne diseases. Even a single cross - X - suggests some kind of health-related aggravation.

It is believed that bad health luck is brought by the winds. So an excellent way of overcoming the double or single X in your Health Luck horoscope is to hang a **wu lou** to appease the winds in your animal sign location.

In 2010, the Sheep is afflicted by the *wu wang* so this can add to any bad health luck indicated in the charts of the Metal Sheep and Water Sheep. So for both of you, it benefits to place a **metal wu lou** as a remedy in your location of SW. This is in addition to the **5 element pagoda** needed to overcome the *wu wang* affliction.

The double circle - OO – against your Health luck suggests that there are no health aggravations at all for you. Those who were sick last year will get better. Good health indications suggest a happy state of mind with no mental aggravations. You have an excellent positive attitude which attracts good fortune. This should make the 55 year old Wood Sheep happy.

Meanwhile the Fire Sheep has a cross and a circle – XO or OX – against its health luck and normally this means there is little cause to worry because the circle overrides the cross, making the year flow smoothly; but because the Sheep is afflicted by the *wu wang* this year, it is advisable to use the **wu lou** and **five element pagoda** cures this year. This should safeguard against any sudden occurrence of a health scare or illness.

Third, Your Finance Luck...

This part of the horoscope reveals the strength and stability of your economic situation in 2010. It also indicates if you can improve your financial situation during the year i.e. whether you can do better than the previous year.

When a double circle - OO – is placed against this luck in your chart, it means that you can gain substantial new wealth in 2010 as is the case with Fire Sheep; and when your chart indicates three circles – OOO – it means your wealth luck is even more certain to materialise. Your business will prosper and whatever expansion you are planning is sure to bear fruit. This is the case with the 67 year old Water Sheep. Remember we have said that Water is the element that is most lacking in 2010, so the double Water element of this Sheep serves him/her very well indeed in the prosperity stakes.

An indication of crosses is a negative reading. The more crosses there are the greater the instability of your financial situation. The double cross – XX – indicates ups and downs in your money luck. Business suddenly takes a downturn and profits can get hit by declines. This is the case with the Wood Sheep who can overcome this bad financial luck indication by making some kind of charitable contribution to ease somebody's financial burden. Generosity is the best antidote to lack of financial good fortune.

Buddhists recommend making offerings to the **White Dzambhala Wealth Buddha** who sits on a dragon, carries the gem spouting mongoose and is attended by four offering goddesses. This is a powerful antidote to counter unstable money luck. If you even have a single cross - X - against your Finance luck, you should not be starting any new business venture or make investments in property or dabble too much in the stock market. You should be extra careful with your funds. Be conservative. A cross with a circle - OX or XO - indicates a stable situation that is neither very bad nor very good.

Fourth, Your Success Luck...

This category puts attention on how well you will do in your career for the year. It offers accurate indications about prospects for promotion and tracks your progress at work, in school or in anything that you may be engaged in doing at the moment. It also gives indications for those still at school, i.e. on their examination luck and affects those involved in a competitive situation. The circles and crosses are a measure of how successful you can be.

When three or two circles - OO – appear, it indicates wonderful recognition and success in all your endeavours; your career, your work, your exams or your performance in any competition. When you have three circles, you attain recognition easily, almost effortlessly, as the year's energy favors you. Two circles mean success with some effort but there is nevertheless success. This is the indication for all those born in the Sheep year in 2010. Hence despite the afflictions of the year, there is still a good dose of positive Success Luck.

Fifth, Your Spirit Essence...

This last category is in many ways the most important as it reveals insights into your inner resilience and chi strength. When the inner essence of your persona is strong and can withstand spiritual afflictions, you can more easily overcome the lack of other categories of luck. When it is weak it makes you vulnerable to the negative effect of various wandering spirits.

While many of these local spirits are harmless, there are some who can be harmful if you inadvertently anger them through saying wrong things carelessly that get picked up by the winds, or desecrating their "homes" such as cutting down old trees or digging up ant hills without proper ritually seeking permission to do so.

These worldly ghosts can only harm those with low levels of Spirit Essence indicated by the crosses. But anyone getting hit by them will get sick and doctors cannot find the cause, yet you can get weaker and weaker. This is the most obvious way of knowing you have been afflicted.

PART 1 - OUTLOOK FOR THE YEAR 2010

A very low spirit essence is indicated by two crosses – XX – and this is the case with everyone born in the Sheep year in 2010. All Sheep born should therefore protect themselves with powerful mantra amulets. Wearing anything with mantras or sutras inscribed on them will protect you from the afflictions of low Spirit Essence.

Sometimes people who dislike you for whatever reason can also use black magic against you. Again these are usually effective only when your spirit essence is low. So once again it is advisable to be careful as your spirit essence shows a XX.

The best protection is to wear protective mantra on your body such as a mantra ring or a powerful seed syllable such as **Hum** or **Om**… these offer powerful protection. You can also wear **mantra pendants** and necklaces in gold, or the powerful protective **Kalachakra pendant**.

Wearing protective mantras on your body can protect you from spirit harm. This Omani pendant is suitable for those with low Spirit Essence in 2010.

PERSONAL LUCK
19 & 79 Year Old Metal Sheep

Type of Luck	Element at Birth affecting this Luck	Element in 2010 affecting this Luck	Luck Rating
Life Force	Earth	Wood	XX
Health Luck	Earth	Wood	XX
Finance Luck	Metal	Metal	X
Success Luck	Fire	Metal	OO
Spirit Essence	Fire	Water	XX

Element influences on the Metal Sheep in 2010

The luck of the Metal Sheep does not look very good in 2010. At a glance, the charts show more crosses than circles, indicating that there is a great deal of negative energy affecting this Sheep. The negativity is more serious for the older Sheep however, as here the threat to its life and health must be taken more seriously than for the younger more vigorous 19 year old Sheep. For the older Sheep, it is advisable to take good care of your health and wear protection at all times. When one is old and all the indications of inner chi essence indicate danger, it really benefits to be mindful of yin forces. Thus best to stay at home, stay rested and do not take risks. It is also not a good year to travel as you are susceptible to picking up all kinds of viruses and bad energy. But for the 19 year old, you have the vitality of youth so you can more eaily overcome the negativities indicated against your Life Force and health. What you need are cures that suppress these indications so you can focus on attaining the kind of success you want. The good news is that you have success luck and although effort is needed to actualise this success, what this means is that you will succeed in whatever you set out for yourself.

The Metal Sheep has confidence in his/her abilities and is likely to be very much in touch with whatever potential lies out there, but there is also a suggestion of vulnerability that makes this person open to losing out on opportunities. There are the annual afflictions to take care of, so it is necessary to ward off the misfortune *wu wang* with good **metal cures** and amulets. The Metal Sheep benefits from the security of familiar surroundings mainly because the Sheep does not have an adventurous streak. The more structured the environment within which this Sheep operates, the better he/she will perform.

7 & 67 Year Old Water Sheep

Type of Luck	Element at Birth affecting this Luck	Element in 2010 affecting this Luck	Luck Rating
Life Force	Earth	Wood	XX
Health Luck	Wood	Wood	X
Finance Luck	Water	Metal	OOO
Success Luck	Fire	Metal	OO
Spirit Essence	Fire	Water	XX

Element influences on the Water Sheep in 2010

The Water Sheep enjoys maximum prosperity and money luck in 2010, fuelled mainly by the Water element of its heavenly stem. There is also an impressive showing of Success Luck. Thus it benefits the 67 year old who owns a business, as the showing on money luck spells either a bonanza appreciation in value of its business or asset, or it indicates a rise in profitability - or both! Those who are retired could see their assets - shares and landed property - going up in value. However and whichever way the luck manifests, it will bring a sense of satisfaction.

This helps to alleviate the afflictions of the year as this Sheep does suffer from a negative showing against its Health Luck. When we read its meaning against the *wu wang* affliction of the Sheep this year, then we realise that there is some cause for concern on the health side. It is thus advisable for this Sheep to stay grounded, ie to not be excessively sociable, or to travel unnecessarily. It is simply not worth it getting hit by air borne germs and viruses in a year which should be bringing satisfaction and happiness. So do be mindful and also wear the right amulets for protection.

In 2010, the popular Water Sheep feels a lack of energy and vitality and cannot seem to keep up with old friends. Relationships tend to be put on hold for most of the year, as the lack of energy and inner strength seems to create hindrances to social interchange.

You are sure to feel this quite acutely so to make up for it, you will need to make the extra special effort to socialise. You need to change your thinking a bit on this matter and actively seek out those you really want to see and interact with. You have the luck to achieve whatever you wish for - socially or professionally - but you also need to make a very special effort.

55 Year Old Wood Sheep

Type of Luck	Element at Birth affecting this Luck	Element in 2010 affecting this Luck	Luck Rating
Life Force	Earth	Wood	XX
Health Luck	Metal	Wood	OO
Finance Luck	Wood	Metal	XX
Success Luck	Fire	Metal	OO
Spirit Essence	Fire	Water	XX

Element influences on the Wood Sheep in 2010

The Wood Sheep's element horoscope chart indicates good success and health luck but is very negative for the other categories. Viewed positively this means that the Sheep will have success this year and also has little to worry about on the health side.

But financial luck is unstable and indeed can be construed to be lacking. There could be moments when money woes creates some real problems and also gives rise to worry and tensions. The Wood Sheep suffers from a lack of water this year. As can be seen from the chart, there is simply no Water at all in its birth set of elements. Thus being a Wood Sheep, all you need is to place physical water in your home to create the presence of water. This is the key to good fortune for you this year, so do go shopping for a very nice water feature that appeals to you.

The Wood Sheep's lack of financial stability is a source of some concern. Placing water is thus crucial for your well being, especially since your Finance Luck is Wood in need of Water. Instead the year's element against this luck is Metal. Here Water not only produces wood but also exhaust the Metal! This is however a Sheep with a good sense of humor. You are both sensible and cool in the face of setbacks and you are the kind who is able to cope well whatever the circumstances. Besides, the Wood Sheep has the good fortune to benefit from his/her own good karma. Those who have demonstrated kindness in the past will find that many of these good deeds will ripen as opportunities for success this year.

Although the Sheep in 2010 has to endure some pretty severe feng shui afflictions, this does not, in the end, immobilise you into failure. You will overcome your own feelings of inadequacy to eventually enjoy success luck, so it is sensible to stay in the game, staying steady and maintaining your cool.

43 Year Old Fire Sheep

Type of Luck	Element at Birth affecting this Luck	Element in 2010 affecting this Luck	Luck Rating
Life Force	Earth	Wood	XX
Health Luck	Water	Wood	OX
Finance Luck	Fire	Metal	OO
Success Luck	Fire	Metal	OO
Spirit Essence	Fire	Water	XX

Element influences on the Fire Sheep in 2010

The Fire Sheep has generally all round good fortune in 2010 despite the double negative against its Life Force and inner Spirit Essence. Thus in terms of financial and work success, there is little to worry. Your health is also showing a stability that suggests little to worry about. However the *wu wang* in the feng shui chart means you still need to arm yourself with good **health amulets** and protection against getting hit by an inconvenient illness hitting you during the year. You benefit from your hidden Fire energy as this bring both success and money luck for you this year. Indeed, the 43 year old Sheep will see the flowering of its own creative flair. This manifesting of your creative side is what will bring you unexpected opportunities that open new pathways for you.

The only problem is that Sheep people are generally less adventurous than most. They also tend to be risk averse, as a result of which some good opportunities could well come and go unnoticed by you!

To make sure this does not happen, it is a good idea to bring in the water feature. Let the wealth-bringing Water element work its magic on you. Place a water feature in the SW of your home or living area and this not only activates your own direction, it will also be activating the indirect spirit of the period (thereby bringing wealth luck).

Do note however that in the Year of the Tiger, the Fire Sheep must curb its impatience and suppress any tendency towards being negative. The lack of energy this year can be frustrating but you need to overcome it; the best way is to use feng shui to jumpstart your vitality luck thereby breaking the negative mental energies of the year. Do not be despairing; instead use your mind to pick yourself up. Cultivate patience and take each day as it comes. Wear **green amber** for extraordinary luck.

31 Year Old Earth Sheep

Type of Luck	Element at Birth affecting this Luck	Element in 2010 affecting this Luck	Luck Rating
Life Force	Earth	Wood	XX
Health Luck	Fire	Wood	OOO
Finance Luck	Earth	Metal	OX
Success Luck	Fire	Metal	OO
Spirit Essence	Fire	Water	XX

Element influences on the Earth Sheep in 2010

The Earth Sheep's luck in 2010 is similar to that of the Fire Sheep except that it has exceptional health luck. In terms of success, this Sheep also enjoys a good outlook for the year. Finance-wise meanwhile, the year appears to be stable - with nothing especially special but also no nasty surprises.

The Earth Sheep is a very practical and optimistic person, excellent with dealing with the realities of life. It is almost as if you expect the path to success to be strewn with stones and boulders. Hence anything that causes you to be forced to slow down or take a detour does not upset you. This is the secret of your success – the ability to adapt and to compromise.

The good news then is that career success is actually very good this year. Professionally and commercially there is much to look forward to and your financial situation will stay quite steady as well.

For those of you who are in working life, do note that this is not a good year to change jobs mainly because you are suffering from the *wu wang* affliction. You also have low chi energy this year so it is better to lean on your good success luck and not rock the boat - at least not this year. Avoid drastic changes because your chi strength cannot sustain changes that are too extreme.

The Earth Sheep will find that 2010 is not a goldmine when it comes to business and economic opportunities. You need to be sharp and alert to spot opportunities. This is the kind of year when you have to study the markets carefully, formulate plans painstakingly and be incredibly patient in the way you manage. For you, however this approach is perfect as te Earth element chi within you automatically gives you a pragmatism that is suitable for this generally tough year. Stay cool and success surely comes.

Part 2
How Sheep Gets On with Others

In Chinese Astrology, your animal sign creates a variety of influences on your life, most significant of which is how it affects the way you interact and get on with the people around you, your partner, your parents, children, siblings, relatives and friends.

Knowing the fundamentals of astrological compatibilities can help you to make your relationships more harmonious, uplifting and definitely less aggravating. You will understand your reactions to people, why you have a natural affinity with some and an instant aversion to others; why some people just annoy you for no reason and why you easily overlook the faults of some others.

PART 2 - SHEEP RELATIONSHIPS

It all boils down to the affinity groupings, the secret friends and ideal soul mate pairings of the Chinese Zodiac! The horoscope compatibility groupings influence how you respond to each of the other eleven signs and explain the special relationships that inherently exist between them.

However, there are annual variations to the level of compatibility amongst animal signs. Everyone's energies, mood, aspirations and tolerance levels change from year to year. People tend to be more or less tolerant, more or less magnanimous or selfish, more distracted or warm depending on how they fare during any year.

When things go smoothly one is better disposed to others and even between two animal signs who are naturally antagonistic, there can still good affinity, enough for two unlikely animal signs to enjoy one another to the extent of becoming temporary soul mates!

Likewise when one is being challenged by a non-stop set of problems, then the slightest provocation can lead to anger even between zodiac friends and allies. That is when friends can become temporary enemies! A falling out between horoscope allies is not impossible.

Hence compatibility between animal signs takes account of time frames. In this section, we look at how the Sheep person relates to others according to specific compatibility groupings, and also how it interacts with the other animal signs in 2010.

Compatibility Groupings

1. Alliance of Allies
2. Paired Soulmates
3. Secret Friends
4. Astrological Enemies
5. Peach Blossom Links
6. Seasonal Trinity

1. Alliance of Allies

There are four affinity groupings of animal signs that make up Alliances of Allies. Each alliance comprises three animal signs who are natural allies of the Horoscope. The three signs within any alliance have similar outlooks and share similar goals. Their attitudes and thought processes are alike, and their support of and compatibility with each other tends to be instant and natural.

When all three animal signs enjoy good fortune in any year, the alliance becomes strong and powerful that year. When there is a natural alliance within a family unit as amongst siblings, or between spouses and a child, the family tends to be very united. They give strength to one another, and when they prosper, good fortune gets multiplied. Families that have alliances of allies are usually extremely close knit. This is one of the secret indications of good fortune. As an alliance, they become a formidable force.

Allies always get along. Any falling out is temporary. They trust and depend on each other and immediately close ranks should there be an external threat. Good personal feng shui comes from carrying the symbolic image of your horoscope allies, especially when they are going through good years.

Ally Groupings	Animals	Characteristics
Competitors	Rat, Dragon, Monkey	Competent, Tough, Resolute
Intellectuals	Ox, Snake, Rooster	Generous, Focused, Resilient
Enthusiastic	Dog, Tiger, Horse	Aggressive, Rebellious, Coy
Diplomatic	Boar, Sheep, Rabbit	Creative, Kind, Emotional

The Sheep and its allies as a group definitely need each other in 2010, and you the Sheep need the others more than they need you. This is because you are afflicted by the Five Yellow and in terms of your Life Force and Spirit Essence, your energies are also at a very low ebb. The best strategy is for you to lean heavily on your allies especially the Rabbit whose luck in 2010 looks reasonably sound.

The phenomenon of the alliance of allies is for those who understand it to seek out each other for support, so that as a group they are able to weather the storms of a challenging year more successfully. Indeed, when the alliance of allies cooperate with each other and team up, their collective energy will get magnified.

Hence if your business associates and you comprise this grouping of Sheep, Rabbit and Boar, the year will be easier to manage. If there are three of you in a family, or within the same department of a company, the Alliance can be activated to benefit every member. In this alliance, the Sheep will naturally lean on the others. Both the Rabbit and the Boar enjoy good star numbers and can provide additional strength.

PART 2 - SHEEP RELATIONSHIPS

For the Sheep, 2010 is when your confidence level drops drastically. You definitely need the help of friends and loved ones. You should also get a hold on yourself and not indulge in excessive feelings of self pity. You have to support your internal negative mind chatter. Stop blaming others and instead focus on being disciplined and determined. You are a naturally generous and compassionate person and you should not let 2010 defeat you.

The Sheep, Boar & Rabbit form the alliance of the Diplomats.

2. Paired Soulmates

There are six pairs of animal signs that can be described as natural soulmates. One sign will be yin and the other yang. In astrology texts, they are described as creating the six Zodiac Houses with each one manifesting its own special niche of compatibility.

The pairing creates a powerful bonding on a cosmic level, and a marriage or business union between any two people belonging to the same Zodiac House will definitely have instant rapport with each other. There will be an inexplicable attraction!

When people talk about 'falling in love at first sight' it is likely they belong to the same House, and should they marry, there is promise of great happiness for them as a family. The soulmates pairing spells happiness in a much more concentrated way than any other kind of zodiac alliance. The yin and yang of the two signs indicate the presence of intrinsic male and female essence that taps into a very special cosmic force.

This combination is also great for those who want to work together professionally – e.g. as business partners in a practice - and between siblings. The mutual strength of each pair is different, as some

Houses of Paired Soulmates

Animals	Yin/Yang	Zodiac House of Creativity	Target Unleashed
Rat	Yang	House of Creativity & Cleverness	The Rat initiates
Ox	Yin		The Ox completes
Tiger	Yang	House of Growth & Development	The Tiger employs force
Rabbit	Yin		The Rabbit uses diplomacy
Dragon	Yang	House of Magic & Sprituality	The Dragon creates magic
Snake	Yin		The Snake creates mystery
Horse	Yang	House of Passion & Sexuality	The Horse embodies male energy
Sheep	Yin		The Sheep is the female energy
Monkey	Yang	House of Career & Commerce	The Monkey creates strategy
Rooster	Yin		The Rooster gets things moving
Dog	Yang	House of Domesticity	The Dog works to provide
Boar	Yin		The Boar enjoys what is created

make better commercial partners than marriage partners. How successful you are as a pair depends on how deeply you bond and how close you allow yourselves to get with one another.

A coming together of yin Sheep with its soulmate the yang Horse creates the *House of Passion & Sexuality*; it is an exciting alliance and together these two animal signs make beautiful love together. As their House name suggests, this is a passionate pair for whom understated sexuality deals some strange cards in 2010. Yes, these two have a special bond although in 2010, the Horse is strong and magnificent while the Sheep is weak, exhausted and insecure. It is important for this couple to balance each other's energies

In 2010 the Horse is full of vigor and vitality while the Sheep has to struggle just to keep up. Passion alone cannot overcome the big mismatch of energy flow for this pair. Should you be in a commercial arrangement with one another, it benefits for the Horse to run the business. Then it is successful! So Sheep, do take note in case you are shacked up with a Horse person or are in partnership with one.

3. Secret Friends
The third set of very special relationships in the zodiac groupings creates the bond of a secret

Pairings of Secret Friends

Rat	Boar	Dog	Dragon	Snake	Horse
Ox	Tiger	Rabbit	Rooster	Monkey	Sheep

friendship under which a very powerful astrological affinity is created. Secret friends are exceptionally compatible. This is a vigorous union of two equals and works very well as a married couple. There is love, respect and goodwill between secret friends. Theirs is a bond which once forged will be hard to break; and even when they themselves want to call it quits with each other, still it will be hard for either party to fully walk away. This pair of signs will stick together through thick and thin. They are fiercely protective of each other and even when they are no longer partners there is still some kind of lingering comradeship and simpatico between them. But one will dominate and it is usually the animal sign whose *heavenly stem* element controls the other.

In the pairing of secret friends, the Sheep is again paired with the Horse. It is obvious there is a strong cosmic bond between these two animal signs despite their unbalanced energies during 2010. The Horse is fiercely loyal as a friend and as a partner so the Sheep is likely to benefit from the Horse's feelings of magnanimity. Generally, Sheep does not manifest the same level of commitment. But as soulmates, a marriage between them promises real happiness. Both are easy going people at heart, so it is likely they will enjoy one another despite the weather.

4. Astrological Enemies

According to the principles of the Horoscope, the animal sign that directly confronts yours is your astrological enemy who can never help you. For the Sheep, the enemy is the Ox. Note that the enemy does not necessarily harm you; it only means someone of this sign can never be of any real help to you. The elements of the two are both Yin Earth, so they tend to be extremely competitive with each other.

Pairings of Astrological Enemies

Rat	Boar	Dog	Rabbit	Tiger	Ox
Horse	Snake	Dragon	Rooster	Monkey	Sheep

There is a six year gap between the two signs and any pairing between them is unlikely to benefit either side. They cannot have sincere intentions towards one another. Marriage between an Sheep and an Ox is unlikely to bring lasting happiness unless there are other indications in their respective paht chee charts. Pairings between arrows of antagonism are usually discouraged by those who investigate Zodiac compatibilities. Sheep are advised to refrain from getting involved with an Ox perosn.

As a business partnership, the pairing is likely to lead to problems, and in the event of a split the separation can be acrimonious even if they start out as best friends. In 2010, any coming together of the Sheep and the Ox will be noisy, argumentative and peppered with quarrels. Better not to take this relationship too far as you will only feel sorry later on.

When two opposite signs have a hostile connection this way and they stay in the same house they cannot be close; they have a completely different sets of friends. If they are siblings, they will not share confidences and will eventually drift apart. If they stay apart, there will not be any direct antagonism, but they are unlikely to have much in common.

The Ox and Sheep are astrological enemies.

5. Peach Blossom Links

Each of the Alliance of Allies has a special relationship with one of the four primary signs of Horse, Rat, Rooster and Rabbit in that these are the symbolic representations of love and romance for one alliance group of animal signs. In the horoscope, they are referred to as *peach blossom animals* and the presence of their images in the homes of the matching alliance of allies brings peach blossom luck which is associated with love and romance.

The Sheep belongs to the Alliance of Sheep, Rabbit and Boar, and they have the Rat as their peach blossom link. The Sheep will benefit from associating with anyone born in the Rat year, and will also benefit from placing a painting or image of a Rat in the North corner of the house, or in the Sheep direction of SW.

The Peach Blossom link of the Sheep person is the Rat. Displaying a good looking Rat image in the North will bring the Sheep person luck in love and romance.

6. Seasonal Trinity

There is another grouping of animal signs which create the four seasonal trinity combinations that bring exceptional luck of seasonal abundance. To many astrology experts this is regarded as one of the more powerful combinations of animal signs. When the combination exists within a family made up of either parent or both parents and with one or more children, they will collectively be strong enough to transform the luck indications for the family members that make up the combination, for the entire year. This means that even when the annual indications of the year may not appear favorable, the existence of the seasonal combination of animals

Seasonal Trinities of the Horoscope

Animal signs	Season	Element	Direction
Dragon, Rabbit, Tiger	Spring	Wood	East
Snake, Horse, Sheep	Summer	Fire	South
Monkey, Rooster, Dog	Autumn	Metal	West
Ox, Rat, Boar	Winter	Water	North

within any living abode is sufficient to transform the luck making it a lot better. The best times will also always be felt by the season indicated by the combination.

It is however necessary for **all three animal signs** to live together or to be in the same office working in close proximity for this powerful pattern to take effect. For greater impact, it is better feng shui if they are all using the direction associated with the

The Snake, Horse and Sheep make up the Seasonal Combination of Summer.

relevant seasons. Thus the seasonal combination of Spring is East, while the seasonal combination of Summer is South.

The Sheep belongs to the seasonal combination of Summer, a combination which strengthens its links with the Horse which is the secret friend of the Sheep. When Sheep and an Horse marry and they have a Snake child for instance, the three of them forms the Trinity of Summer.

This means that they are not only exceptionally close but also attract the luck of the great summer harvest during the summer season! And because they are a summer grouping they tend to be very good looking people.

SHEEP WITH RAT *(Lackluster)*
Boring & Dreary

The Sheep goes through a hard time in 2010, mainly due to the appearance of the Five Yellow in its chart location, but also because the year brings weak energy to it. Horoscope luck is depleting as both Life Force and Inner Essence are lacking. The year also brings setbacks and obstacles. As a result, the Rat gets confusing signals which it finds tedious and discouraging.

> Since these animal signs are not especially compatible, the year 2010 is not an easy year for them as a couple. Life seems to be a monotonous humdrum kind of existence and both are bored with each other.

Sheep's tough year and negative horoscope luck coupled with the affliction of the Five Yellow also discourages the Rat, so that any kind of love relationship between them is likely to be lacklustre and seem insipid and uninteresting. At the same time, it also does not degenerate into something nasty or uncomfortable. But let's face it, the Rat will not be in a any way enchanted by the seemingly insipid Sheep in 2010. What these two want from life differ so much that they will be better off with other partners.

PART 2 - SHEEP WITH RAT

These two animal signs can be dreary and boring with each other and in a year when there is so little affinity between them, then any kind of loving they may find with each other is unlikely to last. They will lack the glue that can bind them permanently. Even in a professional partnership, they are unlikely to last, and if they do, look out for simmering resentments. Both the Sheep and the Rat are good at hiding their real feelings underneath a veneer of false smiles. Scratch the surface however and there can be a minefield of unexploded anger.

The couple that comprise 26 year old Wood Rat and 19 year old Metal Sheep is potentially fraught with misgivings. In the Zodiac, the Rat is flirtatious by nature and the Sheep is coy with opposite sex so this pair will play the mating game, and indulge in a bit of harmless fun. Rat should be careful not to get "hooked" because initial attraction is superficial. The union cannot last.

Between the 26 year old Wood Rat with the 31 year old Earth Sheep the relationship is sure to come under stress, especially with the shadow of the horrible five yellow disturbing this couple. Between the 38 year old Water Rat and the 31 year old Earth Sheep the situation is a little happier, being more even. There is a better chance of the union being happy.

SHEEP WITH OX *(Insensitive)*
Double Negatives Repel

The Ox and Sheep have no attraction for each other, let alone love or have thoughts of a serious commitment. In Chinese astrology, these two are natural adversaries who definitely have little time or sympathy for one another. In 2010, they are equally balanced in terms of what the year has in store for them. They are both Earth people, so there is a down to earth aspect to their personality, but because they are both Yin Earth, the tendency is for them to be constantly negative. And being both negative, there is no attraction, and instead they just naturally repel each other. They have few nice things to say about each other should they be in a relationship. It is all very adversarial.

> In 2010, these two signs have to endure some tough afflictions brought by the feng shui chart of the year. The Sheep is afflicted by the *wu wang* which brings misfortune luck while the Ox is plagued by the illness star. These afflictions do nothing to soften them up for one another, so 2010 does not look good for this pair at all.

Instead of helping one another, they will be aggravating and annoying, adding salt to injury. In fact, 2010 can be the year they split, as any differences between them simply does not go away and will just linger on. Any differences between Ox and Sheep will get magnified quite easily.

In 2010 Ox gets impatient with Sheep's troubles. Being hit by the *wu wang* is not easy, and since this is a major affliction, Sheep does not take kindly to Ox's lack of sympathy. So while Ox is busy changing the world with its grand plans, Sheep prefers to stay quiet and low key and could well walk away from Ox if they are in a relationship. This is probably a good thing to do as the longer term outlook does not look promising to either.

If you are in an Ox/Sheep pairing, you may have endured a difficult time with each other. Living with, or being married to your Zodiac enemy is definitely no fun, and may even hurt you. There is an underlying insensitivity between these two for which there is no real cure. If you have tolerated for many years, there could be aspects of your paht chee charts that make you compatible and if so, then let things be.

Nevertheless, it is always a good idea to wear some kind of **mantra protection** if you are married to your astrological enemy. And place a **large twirling crystal ball** on your coffee table to enhance the increase of good harmony vibes.

SHEEP WITH TIGER *(Aversion)*
In 2010, Feeling Bored

The Sheep has little or no interest in the Tiger in 2010. There is nothing that these two signs have in common that could be the spark for warmer feelings to arise and the year in general is not conducive to them getting together. Sadly, these are two people with so little in common, they would end up finding time spent together to be boring. They might even develop an aversion for one another.

> In certain years, Sheep and Tiger may feel an odd attraction perhaps brought together by some temporary shared interest, but generally they are quite indifferent to one another. In 2010, there is little that can bring this pair together. The energies of the year work against them as a couple.

Sheep knows that Tiger will view it as being too conservative and old-fashioned, but Sheep feels the same way, and views anything with Tiger as lacking the thrill of being in love. Sheep cannot think of doing anything worthwhile together; between them is a great divide and real passion simply cannot arise between them. Sheep is truly convinced that Tiger is not the type of person with whom it can ignite a passionate love affair with. Needless to say, Tiger harbors exactly the same kind of feelings and is

PART 2 - SHEEP WITH TIGER

equally averse to starting anything long term with Sheep. The latter is just more diplomatic, and so Sheep will simply walk away and never bad mouth Tiger. In the eyes of each other therefore, neither will measure up, so it is advisable for them to split rather than waste time on each other. As siblings they will also not be close. Most of the time Sheep's subtlety will be totally lost on Tiger. One tends to be a creature of the wild while the other is more domesticated and would consider itself much more "civilised".

Should these two signs be married, it is likely that Tiger is much older than Sheep. For instance, a match between the 60 year old Tiger would work well with the 31 year old Earth Sheep or the 48 year old Water Tiger might go for the 19 year old Metal Sheep. This has to do with the elements with Sheep's element "producing" Tiger's element!

However, this is an unlikely scenario, because Sheep is definitely not at their best this year. There is the affliction of the Five Yellow which brings troubles. Sheep's horoscope element chart is also very weak. So Sheep is not up to being amiable or sociable this year. Faced with any kind of challenge, Sheep prefers to give up and walk away. Sheep is not in fighting mood this year.

SHEEP WITH RABBIT *(Accommodating)*
Need to Try Harder

In 2010, the very lethargic Sheep needs the support and strong backbone of its friend and ally the Rabbit. If married to a Rabbit person, Sheep is lucky to enjoy the support of its ally. However, despite how positive Rabbit tries to be, Sheep refuses to budge from its pessimism. Sheep is very negative this year, unable or unwilling to see anything good in the Year of the Tiger.

There will be stress in being together, but not anything which Sheep and Rabbit cannot work out. They always do, just that it is aggravating. The 23 year old Fire Rabbit will accept that the 19 year old Metal Sheep tends be negative all the way. Note that you are not much fun to be with this year, so do try to be more accommodating; however, the 31 one year old Earth Sheep has a much better attitude. This Sheep finds the strength to stay upbeat and is able to extract some great openings to end the year on a note of success. This pairing of Rabbit with an older Sheep has a better chance of working out.

In any case, the two are allies of the Zodiac. They get high doing the same sort of things, so their natural compatibility unfolds for them an awareness of their emotional and artistic affinity. This brings them solace and happiness, because in essence, this is what love is about. This couple will behave like soulmates, trusting each other without question and able to go the whole way with each other.

Both are comfortable looking out for the other; there is quiet rapport and comradeship. In 2010 Sheep's restful energy and Rabbit's silent strength find sweet resonance; and despite it being a rather fierce Tiger year, this pair of allies can shut out whatever bad vibes arise and create their own sanctuary.

Any problems that may surface between them will be due to Sheep's afflictive state in 2010, being hit by the Five Yellow. This is the Star of Misfortune and is usually associated with a variety of ills including relationship problems, ill health and a vulnerability to misunderstandings and quarrels.

> Rabbit really needs to very understanding and patient if its partner is a Sheep in 2010. There is no choice but to be supportive. As with last year, Sheep is dependent on its allies for strength, and Rabbit is the stronger of its two allies. This is not the best of years to get together, but if you are already involved, then ride through this year with your partner! In the long term, things always work out well for the both of you.

SHEEP WITH DRAGON (Troubled)
Distracted & Disinterested

These two signs, Dragon and Sheep are not at their best or their strongest in 2010. They are easily exhausted and generally lack the confidence and inner strength to venture beyond the ordinary. Neither has very great interest in pursuing the other and indeed the 19 year old Metal Sheep is totally negative this year.

In terms of the feng shui chart there is the misfortune star to contend with. And the horoscope chart of this Sheep is not any better. This Sheep needs help from other signs to help keep its head above water. The 22 year old Earth Dragon would under normal circumstances be a bit encouraging, but in 2010, turns away, being totally not interested.

The 31 year old Earth Sheep appears perkier to the Dragon and indeed, this Sheep has better luck vibrations which gives it a sense of purpose. This Sheep person can catch the interest of the Fire Dragon if other circumstances are favorable. Otherwise, a romance between them is unlikely. The luck is simply not with them. Should the older of these signs be married to each other, the year will prove listless and discouraging to both.
These are two people who genuinely have an

uncomfortable relationship and the only good news is that they also have little hostility towards one another.

> From Dragon's perspective, it would make sense to focus interest on making the best of the year and this is what it will tend to do. Sheep's survival instincts are also as sharp, so it will use its own resources to bring new meaning into its life. The year is challenging in terms of their relationship with one another, but both will ultimately move on, especially those who are older and more experienced with life.

When Sheep is at its best, it has the capability to attract anyone and capture the attention of even the most disinterested partner, but 2010 seems to be a year which has robbed Sheep of its vitality. It looks like the affliction of the Five Yellow is hitting hard indeed. Sheep is also affected in a negative way by the wrath of the year's Tai Sui. Sad, but the Sheep is going through a hard time this year. However, do not expect Dragon to be sympathetic. Dragon is just not interested enough to be of much help; so Sheep will be left to cope on its own. It is possible that Dragon's attention is elsewhere engaged, being distracted by other interests and in some cases even pursuing other romantic conquests. Dragon could be influenced by the year's *external flower of romance*.

SHEEP WITH SNAKE *(Extremes)*
Blowing Hot & Cold, Yin & Yang

These are the yin and yang signs of the Chinese Zodiac, a trait that is strongly evident in 2010. This is a year when Snake's vitality is at its most dynamic and fired up. Snake is incredibly self assured this year, convinced it can do anything and going all out to prove itself in a broad variety of areas. Snake's sense of adventure is very strong this year. So we can say that Snake's yang energy is burning brightly. Sheep on the other hand registers a double negative in its attitudes. Sheep feels weak where Snake feels strong.

> This should be a complementary pair, but neither sign appreciates what they each consider to be extreme behaviour. Attitudes that surface when they get together are also not to Sheep's liking. Snake comes across too powerful. Sheep meanwhile is thought off as as excessively listless. With such extremes, these two signs are better off with other people.

In any case, there appears little to bind them in a satisfying relationship. Snake will get carried away by how quickly the year seems to move. When on a roll, the days and months fly by or so it will seem to the Snake. Those in the prime of their lives - twenties, thirties and forties - will want to get involved with more exciting people. They will want to enjoy the company of people who are as high as they are, this year; or at least with whom they can do fun thing with.

Even when stuck with someone who seems to be complaining about the year, Snake would prefer "clever" people rather than those who whine and complain without providing a solution. Sheep people have little patience with what they see as the Snake's airs. Any match between them is thus very lacking in affinity and compatibility. If possible it is better if they just split.

In 2010 only the older ones amongst their signs have the patience to live through their relationship. The 67 year old Water Sheep for instance, though suffering from failing health will indulge its Snake partner. The Metal Sheep however cannot be bothered.

From the viewpoint of the Snake, those in their forties, fifties and sixties who are married, the Wood, Water and Fire Snake respectively will not hesitate to fool around. For them the *external flower of romance* could cause them to indulge in outside love interests; and there is nothing much that can be done except for their spouses to install preventive cures to curb infidelity.

SHEEP WITH HORSE *(Steadfast)*
Passionately Supportive

These two signs are secret friends and much more! The Horse and Sheep have a very special connection that transcends time and space and can overcome many different kinds of setbacks and difficulties. The past couple of years have demonstrated this; despite some trying disagreements between them, they are still together, proving how able they are in tolerating adversities brought about by betrayals and mistakes. Somehow being together means too much to them so both will always be reluctant to part. As such, this is one of the most favorable of the Zodiac matches.

In 2010, Horse enjoys a great year while Sheep is hurt by different astrological and feng shui afflictions. There could be loss of income and trying times at work. The Sheep's horoscope is also negative and in need of help. Definitely support from those close and dear is beneficial.

The Sheep that is married to a Horse can rest easy because the auspiciously positioned Horse is there for the Sheep through thick and thin. Horse is extremely steadfast in its support and love for Sheep. Happily, Horse is going through a very good year marked by strong energy and inner assurance. This makes it easy for Horse to lend strong shoulders.

PART 2 - SHEEP WITH HORSE

Horse and Sheep are not just secret friends; they also share the same Zodiac house of sexuality and passion, with the Horse exuding the male yang energy and the Sheep creating the female yin energy. These are the Zodiac terms which mean there is amazing sexual chemistry between the two signs.

> Compatibility would be too tame a word to describe their relationship. They make each other extremely happy irrespective of the time or the place; the conditions or the challenges. In fact, the more problems one has, the more protective the other becomes.

Horse is at its best when in charge and with the gentle Sheep apparently weak and in need of caring, the Horse rises to the occasion. This is exactly the situation with the 20 year old Metal Horse and 19 year old Metal Sheep. There is little doubt that should this young couple meet, they can fall in love and stay close for a long time.

For the 32 year old Earth Horse and the 31 year old Earth Sheep, they are more actively matched as this Sheep can keep up with the Horse. In 2010 both enjoy complementary chi energies and should have a satisfying year together. Those already married will be happy to find that the year brings them closer.

SHEEP WITH SHEEP (Tough)
Hard Time to Stay Upbeat

Those born under the sign of the Sheep have to cope with some very severe feng shui afflictions in 2010; hence they will be distracted and troubled most of the time. This is a sign that generally gets along well with its own sign although they may not be especially passionate about their feelings for each other.

> Sheep tend to be weak and easily influenced. They are sensitive to gossip and tittle tattle so the year becomes more difficult than it should be. They do not interface well with people this year, being easily upset and troubled most of the time; and with their own kind, the Sheep simply ignores the other. They will also be very indecisive in 2010, giving all sorts of excuses for everything.

Sheep people will also put off many things, as there appears to be a reluctance to say or do anything. This listlessness is a result of their weak physical and spiritual strength. The tendency towards indecision can lead to some unsavory results, so problems pile up and the Sheep becomes really impatient with each other. Despite them being alike in many ways, they tend to be blind to the way they are annoying each other. In the Tiger Year, the Sheep and Sheep union is hurt by a double whammy of the year's most severe affliction – the *wu wang* or Five Yellow. There is also the side conflict with the Tai Sui, which makes the Five Yellow more dangerous. In their horoscope element charts, indications stress a great deal of negative luck. Only the young 31 Earth Sheep seem to be recording some real positives in their luck quota.

The 31 year old Sheep will have a better relationship than all other pairings. There is a respectable supply of health, wealth and success luck and this more than make sup for the negative afflictions brought by the feng shui chart to their location,

For the other Sheep couples, the year 2010 could witness difficulties and misunderstandings creeping in to the relationship. Regular disappointments take their toll on this sign and financial and professional setbacks make matters worse so there is a great need for patience and tolerance.

The Sheep couple in their teens and late seventies must be extra careful as luck is on the very low side. In 2010 you need to wear lots of suitable protective amulets that can not only ensure your happiness as a couple, but also block off the year's afflictions.

SHEEP WITH MONKEY *(Nonchalant)*
Indifference Marks This Relationship

These are two animal signs that superficially have little in common, so there is at the start little interest sparked by either one. They could well walk straight past each other with neither registering any interest whatsoever. Not surprising, as they have little in common, being at separate ends of the spectrum of emotions. Their approach to life is different and their personalities differ. So unless there is something special bringing them together, it is unlikely for there to be any attraction between them.

> Even if they are somehow thrown together, initial attraction does not last. Sheep might have a secret crush on Monkey, or Monkey could find Sheep seductive, but interest in each other will not last long. Both sides will get easily distracted by others. And definitely do not expect there to be any grand passion between them.

The 2010 Tiger Year is much kinder to Monkey than to Sheep, as a result of which, luck for the Sheep is so much worse off than the Monkey even though they both have to cope with the Five Yellow affliction which brings misfortunes. This affliction hits them both with different levels of severity. Sheep gets hit a lot worse!

PART 2 - SHEEP WITH MONKEY

The difference is due to their pattern of elements. Monkey is strong, Sheep is weak. There is a powerful vitality emanating from Monkey's aura, while Sheep is listless and easily exhausted. Sheep is sure to be hurt by Monkey's tendency towards insensitivity. Monkey takes the submissive Sheep very much for granted; so Sheep feels ignored causing it to withdraw into its shell. This creates the danger of things getting into a downward spiral for this pair.

In 2010, the 18 year old Water Monkey is riding high, with the energy of the year bringing plenty of good fortune. Should they be married, Sheep will resent this obvious difference. As Sheep will find it hard to keep up with Monkey, there is danger that Monkey could look outside the marriage for some fun and games. So for Sheep, this imbalance of energy between the two of you has the potential to bring heartache and worries.

Sheep finds it hard to keep up with the Monkey; stress and strains impact on their marriage. The best advice for the Sheep is for it to ride through the year. The less said and done, probably the better. However, the 31 year old Earth Sheep paired with the 30 year old Monkey can stay abreast with the Monkey. With the 43 year old Fire Sheep, the relationship favors the Sheep.

SHEEP WITH ROOSTER (Distant)
Rubbing Each Other up the Wrong Way

The Sheep and Rooster do not like one another very much and no matter how hard they try, nothing can make either feel warm thoughts for the other. Between them is a great divide, and it is because secretly, they do not think much of each other. Sometimes they find it hard to hide their feelings, but most times, they make sure to keep a distance between them so there is no need to interact or put up with one another. When too close, they tend to rub each other the wrong way.

The Sheep has an aversion to the Rooster whom it considers to be arrogant and too superior by far... to the gentle Sheep, Rooster is bossy and critical and thinks too much of itself. The Rooster meanwhile has no opinion about the Sheep. Everything is bland and boring as far as the loud and perky Rooster is concerned. So at best, this will be a superficial friendship. Should these two marry and start a life together, life is one long drag. Disappointment is sure to manifest. Hostility and resentment easily creep into the relationship, causing unhappiness.

In 2010 the situation between these two is distinctly chilly. This is a year when Roosters are stronger than usual, and as a result, becoming unbearably domineering. To Sheep, Rooster is impossible to handle, especially as it has its own sets of afflictions and problems to deal with. Between them there is neither empathy nor rejoicing. Sheep cannot be happy for Rooster's good fortune and Rooster cannot feel any sympathy when it sees Sheep suffering as a result of the year's troubles.

> The married couple will go their separate ways with Rooster straying away from the marital bed and Sheep not caring enough to put up a fight. Rooster could start an affair, succumbing to the flower of external romance star, and Sheep might find comfort in someone else's arms.

In 2010, Rooster's energy is stronger than that of Sheep and in a pairing of the 29 year old Metal Rooster with the 31 year old Earth Sheep, Sheep gets overshadowed by Rooster's vitality but happily enjoys some good success luck. This couple have no problems doing their own thing. The Sheep married to the 41 year old Earth Rooster is unimpressed by Rooster's success; but 53 year old Fire Rooster is both successful and better natured in 2010, and thus more bearable. The 65 year old Wood Rooster has great success luck and is mellowed by age and the Sheep married to this Rooster will find things go better than the other Sheep/Rooster couplings.

SHEEP WITH DOG *(Sympatico)*
Strengthening Each Other

In 2010, should the eligible Sheep meet an available Dog person, sparks may fly between them as they instinctively find comfort in each other's company. While not madly compatible, the Sheep and Dog find a restful solace being together. These two are gentle, loyal people who gravitate towards each other quite naturally. Here, it is a case of two people turning to a like-minded person in a tough year.

The Year of the Tiger is going to be challenging for both Sheep and Dog as they have their share of afflictions to contend with. The unlucky Sheep especially has to cope with setbacks brought by the *wu wang* or Five Yellow; and Dog will be suffering from low energy levels.

But it is not all bad news; there are also good moments of high bliss for both during the year. The 28 year old Water Dog for instance has some great financial luck coming its way, brought by the Small Auspicious Star from the 24 Mountains. This gives Dog the confidence to go out in search of someone to get entangled with. Should it meet up with the 31 year old Earth Sheep, they will complement one another in the best possible way. These two will then find the year to be very encouraging for them to be together. The 40 year old Metal Dog is not quite as lucky, but for this Dog, pairing up with the 31 year old Sheep will help it overcome much of the challenges of the year.

> Sheep and Dog are people who do not possess super strong personalities; they are not doormats, but neither are they loud or quick to anger. They are people who are easy going and sensitive to others. So a pairing between them becomes a stable relationship that can stand the test of time.

However, do not expect grand passion to develop as neither can inspire that kind of love for the other. Passion for the Sheep is found with the Horse; and for the Dog, with the Monkey or Rooster. You actually have something better and far more secure and unwavering. So be assured that for you, commitment is the real thing.

In a love relationship, this pair works well. In a professional partnership however, Dog may find Sheep fickle and Sheep finds Dog indecisive. But as a couple, they are popular with lots of friends. Life together is pleasant and also quite sociable. The only problem this year is to resist the urge to be pessimistic. To be happy, it is better to distract the mind and go for holiday than to worry too much.

SHEEP WITH BOAR *(Favorable)*
Romance & Comfort with your Ally

The Sheep goes through a troubled year but finds solace and comfort with its astrological ally, the Boar. Well suited and compatible, this couple enjoys a natural affinity that transcends the setbacks of daily life. In 2010, both experience the good and bad of the Tiger Year with Sheep feeling the brunt of it. But with the help of Boar, Sheep survives 2010 with a sense of humor. Sheep feels fortified and practical as ever, because there is love enough to help Sheep make it through the nights.

> What this pair enjoys is a relaxed and easy relationship, the kind of comfort level which make them true soulmates. They experience joy in each other's company and can also forge a work relationship that is both supportive and helpful. There is a partnership that works with little effort and should they be married to one another, it is a happy union. They will make it easily through the Tiger Year.

This is because the Sheep and Boar make up two thirds of the group of allies that are described as the Diplomats of the Zodiac. They share a love of the gentle lifestyle which mirrors their desire for a life of quiet elegance. They communicate on similar wavelengths and are sensitive of each other's needs and feelings.

Should the young 19 year old Metal Sheep get together with the 27 year old Water Boar, the attraction will be instant, with Boar taking the lead, guiding and caring for Sheep all the way. This will be a beautiful match, with Sheep bringing out all the protective instincts of Boar. They will be inseparable in 2010.

The 31 year old Earth Sheep meanwhile enjoys a strong set of elements which brings great health, moderate financial and good success luck. This Sheep does better with the 27 year old Water Boar but has just as good a rapport with the 39 year old Metal Boar.

For the older Sheep and Boar people, the year brings a variety of luck patterns that make it easy for them to complement each other. Generally however, Boar has a stronger and more auspicious year than Sheep. Nevertheless, there is excellent synergy between them and through the year, just by being together, they will find many of the disappointments a lot easier to cope with. They are thus excellent for one another.

Part 3
Sheep's Monthly Horoscope 2010

The coming year will be a challenging one for the Sheep person. There is the affliction of the Five Yellow to contend with as well as low energy and vitality levels. Bad luck can strike at any time, so it is of great importance this year to think of protection first before enhancement. There may be good moments, but first you have to shelter yourself from harm.

Watch for the months when your luck is at a particularly low ebb, and make it a point to arm yourself with the correct talismans and cures. Business luck is difficult with all kinds of obstacles threatening to crop up. There may be falling out with friends or partners. Amidst hard times, the Sheep must stay strong and determined. Wear or carry the **Five Element Pagoda** this year.

1ST MONTH
February 4th - March 5th 2010

BUSINESS & PROFITS LUCK VERY GOOD

The start of the year looks promising with good business luck in store. Things started this month will have better than average chance of success, so make it a point to keep busy to make the most of your fortunes while the wealth star pays you a visit. Auspicious Earth chi dominates your luck this month, which helps to strengthen your personal energy. Money luck is good. However, while business luck is promising, there are hidden dangers, so don't take anything for granted. Do your checks and due diligences when entering into something new. At work, beware of secret rivals. While you can afford to be braver this month, don't forget to watch your back.

WORK & CAREER – *Office Politics*

While money and income luck is good, workplace developments could present challenges. Jealous colleagues could be plotting against you behind your back, whether consciously or not. You may have to deal with sarcastic comments or put-downs from middle management, especially if the big bosses seem to like you. Protect yourself at work by wearing a **golden Rooster**. This will quell office politics directed your way. While you may have many good ideas, think everything through before revealing them, or they could be stolen from under your nose. There will be some obstacles in your path this month, but if you put your mind to overcoming them without getting flustered, success will be yours in the end.

BUSINESS – *Many Opportunities*
The Sheep in business will have many opportunities this month. You can pick any one of them and make something good of them. But if you are thinking of going into a joint venture, make sure you trust your partner, because starting out on the wrong foot will not bode well for the partnership. Even if the opportunity appears too good to miss, if you don't like the people involved in the deal, it is not worth going ahead with. Business for you right now is all about the people. Work with the right people and everything will go right; work with the wrong people and everything is bound to go wrong.

LOVE & RELATIONSHIPS – *Opposite Attact*
Opposites attract this month so don't close your mind to unusual types. Single Sheep could end up falling

head over heels with the most unlikely of partners, if only you give things a chance to develop. Don't let first impressions count for too much or you could miss an incredible opportunity to be with someone you could well end up with for the long term. In general, relationship luck is very good this month, particularly on the romantic front. If you are already married, your spouse will provide you with plenty of emotional support and encouragement this month. If you reciprocate the gesture, your union could well blossom to a new and much deeper level.

HEALTH & SAFETY – *Be More Careful*
There are indications that there is danger of injuries to the joints and limbs. Sheep people who are involved in highly physical sports should be more careful this month. Take it easy. Wear or carry a **Wu Lou** to ward off illness and accidents.

SCHOOL & EDUCATION – *Exam Luck*
Education luck is excellent this month, so make the most of it by putting aside enough time for revision. Those sitting exams will fare well. Round off your daily routine by making sure you get fresh air and exercise. Although it is good to want what you want with a passion, remember it is just as important to have balance in life. Keep things in perspective and everything will work out well for you.

2ND MONTH
March 6th - April 4th 2010

DANGER OF ACCIDENTS AND MISHAPS

The Five Yellow combines with the number 7 star to cause loss and misfortune happenings. There may be violent eruptions for some Sheep born, so don't let any argument become too heated. There is disharmony at work and at home. You may find you have a shorter fuse, and that it is more difficult to get along with people. Your horoscope takes its toll on your relationships. You need to work harder than usual to maintain the goodwill you have carefully built up over time. Refrain from listening to outsiders. Learn to trust your own instincts but at the same time, don't reveal your true feelings to others or you risk offending the wrong person. Lay low this month and maintain a lo profile. Carry a protective amulet like a **brass mirror** to deflect away bad chi coming your way.

WORK & CAREER — *Power Play*

If you feel you've reached your peak in the job you're currently holding, it is better to wait till next month before contemplating any major change in your professional life. Your feelings may be transient ones and you don't want to make any decisions you might regret later on. If you are in a competitive working environment, there could be some power play in the office. For color choice, wear blues and blacks, which will make you stronger this month. This will also ensure you can take on any competition you face.

BUSINESS – *Trust Your Instincts*
You may have to face a dispute with a business partner over money matters, but before jumping to conclusions, investigate thoroughly before making false accusations. Don't listen to gossip from meddling third parties; they may have an alternative agenda and could cause an unneccesary fall-out between yourself and your business associates. Think through your decisions carefully before making them. Trust your instincts; you have good intuitive luck this month and should have confidence in your own reasoning.

LOVE & RELATIONSHIPS – *Supportive Partner*
Sheep people in steady relationships will find their partners extremely supportive this month. Sometimes your partner may offer an opinion you don't immediately agree with, but take what is said seriously as there may be some valid points. The romance is there but it is not scorching; rather, it is

gently simmering under the surface. This month you will find love of the warm and cosy kind, rather than the wild, uncontrolled passion you may crave.

HEALTH & SAFETY – *Avoid Late Night Out*

Watch out for a possible mouth-related illness. This could also mean sickness via food poisoning. Try not to expose yourself to infectious viruses this month or put yourself at risk. As you have the violent star in your chart, lady Sheep should be more cautious when out and about. Avoid staying out too late and carry a **Night Spot Protective Amulet** to keep you safe.

SCHOOL & EDUCATION – *Productive*

For the young Sheep pursuing his/her studies, this will be a productive month if you put in the time and the effort. Try not to compare yourself to others. Judge your own success by how much you've improved rather than by how well you're doing compared to your peers. In the end, good results come about from conscientiously hard work. Overcomparing will just get you feeling down or inadequate, not the best ingredients for a top student!

3RD MONTH
April 5th - May 5th 2010

FINANCIAL LUCK BROUGHT BY INFLUENTIAL MAN

This month is characterized by helpful people who materialize in your life just as you need them. Your mentor figure could be someone very close to you on a personal level or it could be someone more connected than you who can help you in your career by opening doors. The person helping you is likely to be a man of influential standing. Be industrious. The more hardworking you are, the more you can benefit from the help that's on offer to you. Always be humble when accepting help from others. When opportunities present themselves, move quickly to benefit from them. Maintain a sense of urgency when following up on leads and let your instincts guide you. Things unfold very pleasantly in your life right now so you can afford to be bold in your decisions.

WORK & CAREER – *Forging Relationships*

If you manage to catch the eye of the right person this month, you can fast track your success. If you are going to put in extra effort, let some of it go into forging a good relationship with your boss. But you also need to get along with your colleagues, so don't neglect these relationships either.

It pays to network this month. You feel comfortable around others and even if you find it difficult to find common ground with someone you ought to be cultivating as an ally, don't lose hope; it will come. Keep up your genius and you can achieve a lot this month.

BUSINESS — *New Ideas*
Good business is all about good management this month. If you can successfully motivate the people you work with, you are already there. Don't be afraid to try out new ideas. When it comes to strategy, the more brains the better, so encourage the people who work with you to participate in brainstorming. You'll be surprised how successful a couple of productive meetings can be. Involving the others in the strategic part of the business will also improve loyalty and enthusiasm.

LOVE & RELATIONSHIPS — *Romantic!*
You may be feeling unusually romantic, but there is no harm in letting yourself be flighty and frivolous once in a while, especially when it comes to love. If you are tense or hesitant about showing your

feelings, you could miss out on something really good Sometimes you need to take risks and put yourself on the line if you truly want to get somewhere in the romance and relationships stakes.

FRIENDSHIPS – *Beware Sweet Talkers*
Your friendship may be sought out by others who want something from you. While many seek you out because they genuinely like you, there may be one or two who have their own agenda. Beware the sweet talking mentor. He or she could enter your life as someone promising to help you out in your career, fuelling your dreams of making it big in the corporate world. Poison can lie hidden amongst sweet words. To protect against unsavory persons entering your life, wear a **protective mantra**. This will repel those with bad intentions away.

SCHOOL & EDUCATION – *Mentor Luck*
A promising month lies in wait for young Sheep students pursuing their studies. You find it easy to motivate yourself. A mentor figure could enter your life making everything you study seem so much more interesting. When you start to enjoy what you're working on is when you'll discover the wonders of learning. Doing well is not a problem and those of you sitting for tests or exams this month will likely do very well.

4TH MONTH
May 6th - June 5th 2010

GOSSIP AND SLANDER BRING WORRIES
Arguments threaten to get out of hand this month. You could be betrayed by people you trust. Troublemakers surface at work. Others may gossip behind your back, or even openly in the news and media if you are a high profile person. This is a dangerous month for you when things threaten to get critically bad. Wear the **Fire Gold amulet** faithfully. Don't crack under the pressure. If things get to be too much, it may be best to pack your bags and go on holiday. Remove yourself from the strains and hassles of everyday life. You may be in need of a good recharge and a vacation away could do you a world of good.

WORK & CAREER – *Misunderstandings*
Be prepared to hit a few snags at work. Misunderstandings with colleagues could become rather more frequent than you would like. Things are not going to be easy this month. There is no substitute for hard work, so be prepared to slog it if you're working towards a promotion this year. There are new challenges to face each day, but these

challenges are the pathways to new possibilities in your career. Don't let small hiccups distract you from the big picture. This month it is better to stick with the status quo. Leave any bravado for another time.

BUSINESS – *Take The Initiative*
In work and business, you have to take initiative. Lying idle will see the competition overtake you. Whether things happen for you after taking the initiative is a different story, but bide your time and your efforts now will soon bear fruit. Be alert to everything that's going on around you. Your powers of observation will reap its rewards. Refrain from spending too much money; instead, focus on making money for now. Improvements that require capital expenditure can wait. For now you want to be liquid.

LOVE & ROMANCE – *Enjoy Your Bacherlorhood*
This month is better when it comes to relationships. While your work and career may bring you heartache and worry, the scenario is happily different when it comes to your personal life. Sheep who have a solid family life will tend to do better this month than their fellow single Sheep. You feel better when you are around people who genuinely care for you.

For the single Sheep, new romances may have to wait till next month before crystallizing. If you have your eye on someone, hold back the big moves. If you hook up with someone this month, chances of them being good for you are slim, and breaking up the relationship later will be difficult. Enjoy bachelorhood for now and party with a group of friends instead. If you're not the partying kind, curl up with a good book.

HEALTH & SAFETY — *Avoid The SW*

Watch the double misfortune stars in your chart this month. If you feel under the weather and in need of a medical checkup, don't keep putting it off. Your health could deteriorate more quickly than you think. Stress-related illnesses could take their toll. Maintain a good balance in your life. Elderly Sheep suffering from high blood pressure should be particularly careful this month. Avoid spending too much time in the SW sector this month. Install a large **5 Element Pagoda** here to counter the strong afflictions the month brings.

EDUCATION — *Average*

There are no major events when it comes to your studies this month. This is an average month when you are not feeling your best. Bide your time till next month which will be particularly good for student Sheep.

5TH MONTH
June 6th - July 6th 2010

ROMANTIC ENTANGLEMENTS BRING DISTRACTIONS

This month brings danger in the form of romantic entanglements. Beware of illicit affairs and romances. Misfortune lurks in new encounters. It is important not to give in to temptations of the heart. A wrong move no matter how seemingly innocent could end in tragedy and heartache. You are easily distracted this month and will have to work hard to stay focused. Try to do so, because it is important. There is bad luck for young men, who should watch their step. Life could change in a moment, so don't let a moment's weakness cause you to slip up.

WORK & CAREER – *Stay Low Profile*

This is not a good month to poke your nose where it doesn't belong, or to bite off more than you can chew. Stick to what you are responsible for at work and resist the temptation to involve yourself in other people's business. Stay low profile this month and let the bad chi dissipate as the month passes. Wear gold to overcome the inauspicious energies. Danger comes in the form of temptation of the romantic kind. Avoid office romances with a ten foot pole. They spell bad news. Avoid working too late with just one other colleague. Once you get involved, it will be hard to extricate yourself before you do permanent damage to your job, marriage and life.

BUSINESS — *Making Friends*
Your strength is in making friends this month. You don't need to work in a team to increase your sales or to secure new accounts. In fact you may be luckier if you do it alone this month. You do well as front man, so get out there yourself rather than relying on others this month. There is a sense of authority about you, which makes others feel confident with your ability. Sell yourself. A little arrogance, as long as it is not taken too far, never did anyone any harm. Danger this month however comes from scandal. Do not get involved romantically with anyone you're not supposed to be with. Rumors spread like wildfire, and you do not want to give your adversaries ammunition against you.

LOVE & RELATIONSHIPS — *Danger of Scandal*
For the single Sheep, this is a month full of social and romantic opportunities. You boast a hectic social life, and the fuller your social calendar, the happier you are. However, beware the danger of scandal

this month. Avoid getting involved with married individuals, or people you're not supposed to be with, like your boss. Your love life is promising as long as you stick to some socially accepted protocols.

Those of you who are married need to be a bit careful this month. The Star of External Romance threatens to wreak havoc in your comfortable idyll. Wear the double happiness symbol or carry one as a charm to avoid a third party entrée to stir trouble in your marriage.

EDUCATION – *New Discoveries*
This is a month that favors the scholar. Students and those involved in research will find their concentration levels improve. Discoveries can be made and breakthroughs in research possible. Those sitting for exams are likely to do very well indeed, but you can carry a pagoda amulet to improve study luck.

However, although your mind power is superior this month, it is easy to get distracted. For the 20 year old Sheep, romance and matters of the heart beckon. If you are serious about your studies, don't get too heavily involved with anyone just right now. Leave romance and relationships for another time, or at least until all exams are over. You don't want to jeopardize what could be.

6TH MONTH
July 7th - Aug 7th 2010

SHEEP ENERGY WEAKENS THIS MONTH
Gossip continues, wearing the Sheep down. Your energy weakens and you find yourself wither in the face of criticism. Strenuously avoid getting involved in a fight, engaging in arguments or losing your temper. **Wear red** and gold to quell the quarrelsome energies of the month. Overcome slander and back biting with a **Fire Sword** – place in the SW sector this month. While you may find yourself having the knack of getting into situations which make your blood boil, stop yourself from lashing out in anger. You will only hurt yourself and maybe those who love. Your enemies will have to be defeated another way.

WORK & CAREER – *Peacemaker*
Work is not smooth this month. Misunderstandings and differences of opinion could make time at the office more stressful than it should be, but you will only compound matters if you insist on retaining stubbornness and inflexibility. Don't make unnecessary enemies. Even if you know you are better

than your rival at work, avoid facing off with him or her and certainly don't publicly embarrass your co-workers when you don't need to. If a co-worker is acting strangely, talk to him or her. You want your differences out in the open and sorted out. Don't allow anyone to harbor ill feelings towards you. You don't need that kind of aggravation now. Make yourself and active peacemaker and you'll soon find things going your way again.

BUSINESS – *Team Work*
Avoid closing deals or doing big business this month. New initiatives set in motion last month can go ahead, but don't have any major changes in direction right now. Your intuition may fail you and your instincts are not as sharp as usual, so let others steer the ship for a while. This is a good time to build up your generals because you can't run the business in a way that requires your full attention the whole time. Build up a team you can trust is more important.

There may be legal tribulations to deal with. Trouble with the authorities may cause much stress. However, don't try to sort things out this month when your luck has taken a dip. Wait it out unless you can reach a mutual conciliatory action. But don't engage yourself in a fight of any kind, because you are more than likely to lose.

LOVE & ROMANCE – *Wear Reds*
Heartaches are a distinct possibility this month, so it may be better to focus elsewhere in your life. If you are looking for a happy relationship with your better half, be prepared to make some sacrifices. The fighting chi is quite overpowering this month and most of it originates from you. Wear plenty of reds to counter the hostile chi affecting you. Don't give false ultimatums. Your partner may just take you seriously and you'll end up the loser.

For the single Sheep looking for romance, there is no harm in flirting or having some fun, but if it is something serious you're looking for, you may have to look a bit longer.

EDUCATION – *Feeling Rebellious*
Inner turmoil threatens to disturb the peace this month. You may be feeling a little rebellious with an urge to break loose from your chains. At the same time, your Sheep nature reminds you of your responsibilities. If you find yourself wanting to break free, remind yourself about your ultimate goals for the future, and just make sure you don't do anything to jeopardize the future you have planned for yourself.

7TH MONTH
Aug 8th - Sept 7th 2010

GRAVE DANGER OF ILLNESS
Watch out for your health. The illness star flies into your chart to join the misfortune star, threatening to sap your energy and make you more susceptible to viruses. You're also more accident-prone this month, so take care of yourself and don't subject yourself to anything dangerous like rough sports or driving dangerously. Carry a **Wu Lou amulet** in your purse or pocket at all times to keep sickness at bay. Elderly or sickly Sheep people should take more care this month.

Money seems to flow out faster than it comes in this month. If you're feeling poor, don't spend so much! Cut back on things you don't need. This does not mean you should scrimp and save but it does mean you shouldn't spend money like water.

WORK & CAREER – *Mend Fences*
While you may find work relationships unfriendly this month, it is important to make the effort to cultivate good relationships with your colleagues. You

may not have much in common in terms of outside interests, and may not be bosom pals when it comes to what you do have in common, but you're going to need allies in the next few months. Alienating yourself won't do you any good if you're planning on staying in your present job for the long haul. You may also need to mend some tattered relationships from the explosive chi of last month.

As long as you use your "meek Sheep" persona, others will fall for your charm and you will find it easy to make friends. You might also need someone to cover for you one of these days, especially if your health takes a beating from the illness star hovering in your chart. Start making friends!

BUSINESS – *Be Meticulous*
Wealth luck is down and you find it more difficult to close deals and make money. Sales may be much slower than usual and inspiration trickles in slowly. You're probably going to find it difficult to be creative this month, so don't hope to hatch grand ideas. Instead, focus on pure old-fashioned hard work. You're going to have to put in the hours if you want to do well this month. Be meticulous in everything. Missing a small detail could prove costly indeed. Big ideas should be reserved for another time. Be prepared to do some effective delegating if you find

the illness star catching up with you. While there is a lot to get done, strike a balance between work, play and rest, or you could burn out in the process.

LOVE & RELATIONSHIPS – *Communicate*
While luck is down elsewhere, Sheep people with supportive partners will find their other half a tremendous source of support this month. Be open with your partner. If you are facing problems, share them. They will be able to help you. Holding back at this time will only drive a wedge between the two of you. Being secretive is worst of all. This could lead to jumping to conclusions that could be harmful to your relationship.

FRIENDSHIPS – *Learn to Listen*
You are in great need of friends this month. Obstacles you face could get you down, but don't let your worries cause you to become snappy with the very people who want to help you. If you ask for their advice, be prepared to listen. You may have the tendency to react positively only when they tell you what you want to hear. But if you find yourself getting like this, stop asking for their opinion.

Place a Wu Lou next to your bed to protect your health in August when the illness star strikes.

8TH MONTH
Sept 8th - Oct 7th 2010

OBSTACLES DISSOLVE AND LUCK IMPROVES

Your luck improves this month and work-related obstacles ease up. The business scenario is still challenging but there is light at the end of the tunnel. There is small success indicated and whatever hard work you put in will start to pay off. In general you will find things start to go more smoothly.

You can expect some significant turning points in your life this month. While certain changes may jolt you out of your comfort zone, you will come to be pleased with the change. Any fear of the unknown will ease up once you discover things are become better and brighter for you. The future starts to look clear again but you must stay focused for any real success to materialize.

WORK & CAREER — *Small Auspicious*

Organize your work well because there will be many things to juggle. Learn to work under pressure without letting your work quality slip. This month your energy is renewed. Continue to develop rapport with your boss. Aim to impress this month. You have Small Auspicious luck which means there is something good waiting for you in the pipeline. The more of an impact you make now, the better your prospects for the future. The next few weeks will give you a good chance to prove your worth. Make the most of it before the opportunity passes you by.

BUSINESS – *Hidden Catches*

Luck in business is promising this month. You may be in with a chance to broker the deal of your life. But before you celebrate, watch out for hidden catches. You probably won't get everything you want and obstacles could pop up which threaten to sour the deal. Trust your instincts on what you can compromise on and what you can't. You have the benefit of luck on your side, so chances are things will end up a success. But you'll need confidence in large doses if you're going to push the deal through.

LOVE & RELATIONSHIPS – *Don't Play Games*

When it comes to love, things happen quickly this month. If you're not currently romantically involved, you can expect that to change very soon. Suitors are aplenty and there may be more than one you have your eye on! But if you're looking for something serious, don't play games. Juggling hearts only lead to complications that you don't need in your life.

For the Sheep person already in a steady relationship, you may start to look on your partner differently. They could be more caring or more romantic this month. Things get more exciting between you and passion returns in a new guise. Make time for romance no matter how busy you get. Life is good right now and can be a whole lot better if you let your heart do some of the talking.

HOME & FAMILY – *Refresh The Chi*
This is a good month to do some spring cleaning and to refresh the energy of your home. Throw out old things you don't need any more to make space for new things to come into your life. This is an ideal time to renovate and make changes to your home. A fresh coat of paint or a change of carpet will do wonders to renew the chi energy in your home.

You benefit also from some changes to your personal routine. Take up a new hobby, learn a new skill, try something new. It could open up whole new avenues for you in your life. It would also do you good to make some new friends away from your current circle.

9TH MONTH
Oct 8th - Nov 6th 2010

CHALLENGES START TO MOUNT

Your luck from last month dissipates quickly and challenges start to mount. Old problems resurface causing some stress and worry. Watch you don't overdo your spending this month as you could quite easily get carried away. Keep an eye on cash flow and try not to buy things on impulse. Definitely avoid speculating and gambling. Sheep in business suffer setbacks. Watch for hidden dangers this month. Remain alert so that surprises do not catch you out. Life may get more complicated, but don't let things get to you. If you stop worrying and start planning, you will get through the month in one piece.

WORK & CAREER — *Fierce Competition*

You may face some fierce competition at work. This is not the time to take on a challenge openly, but we aware of the goings-on around you if you want to outsmart your rivals. While you may not see things in a competitive like, if your rivals at work do, you're going to find yourself dragged in if you continue to harbor ambitions up the career ladder. Get yourself

PART 3 - MONTHLY OUTLOOK : OCTOBER

a **Victory Horse** to triumph over the competition. The Horse is also your ally and secret friend; having an image of a victory horse on your desk or near you will also activate horoscope ally luck, turning your adversaries into your allies. While things may get cutthroat at work, be careful not to overdo things or you could make yourself sick with exhaustion. Be sure to allow yourself time to recharge, if not during the week, then at weekends.

BUSINESS — *Stay Positive*

Try to stay positive this month even if things don't seem to be going as smoothly as you'd like. You may be confronted with problems of all kinds, from staff problems to cash flow worries. There are likely to be many challenges to face, causing you to lose some confidence. Some of the decisions you take may not turn out to be

Display a Victory Horse on your workdesk to triumph over your rivals ta work. This will also turn your adversaries into allies.

good ones, but take everything in your stride and look on it as a useful lesson. Your luck is down this month, so you'll have to put in double the effort; but at the same time, cut yourself at least double the slack. Beating yourself up over mistakes won't get you anywhere. But if you can learn from them, then you could turn a challenging month into a productive one.

LOVE & RELATIONSHIPS – *In Demand*

You have a lot more confidence this month when it comes to dating and relationships than you do in your professional life. Enjoy yourself. The month is not all bad, and in terms of your social life, it's there if you want it. You are just as in demand as ever when it comes to invitation lists. Everyone wants you at their party, it is just whether or not you want to go. You may not feel up to it, but getting out and about might be just what you need to lift your spirits.

The month won't go well for you if you lose your spunk; in fact, that's what your luck is hinging on right now. Get that fighting attitude back and things will improve for you considerably. For the married Sheep, lean on your spouse for support if you need; you'll be surprised at the gems of advice they can give you.

10TH MONTH
Nov 7th - Dec 6th 2010

MONEY LUCK RETURNS BUT OTHERS CHALLENGE YOU

Earth chi dominates your chart this month, which brings both good and bad. There is some money luck but some loss is also possible. This is certainly not a time to be overly confident when it comes to risk-taking, but you can be braver than you have been this past year. Your luck has improved and things finally start going your way. However while business and wealth luck picks up, so do competitive pressures.

At work you may receive mixed signals, and for those of you managing a team, there could be challenges to your authority. If you want to remain where you are, stand firm. The Sheep person who is strong will prevail this month, so make sure you conjure up enough inner strength to overcome your rivals. Remember, don't give your trust to others too easily, there may be a backstabber in your midst.

PART 3 - MONTHLY OUTLOOK : NOVEMBER

WORK & CAREER – *Think Things Through*

Opportunities open up for you when it comes to your career. Some of you may receive an alternative job offer while others of you may have been scouting around for something different. Before you make the decision to leave for greener pastures, think through things carefully. Whether you stay or change jobs is immaterial; both can be good decisions. However, it is important to trust your own judgment. Follow your own instincts. Don't let anyone else talk you into something you are uncomfortable with. But once you make a decision, stick with it. No regrets!

BUSINESS – *Follow Your Instincts*

Wealth luck is promising this month, but pursuing great wealth alone may be difficult. This month bodes well for well-matched partnerships. If there is a mutually beneficial joint venture, go for it. But when picking your business partner, only go into business with someone you trust and someone you are comfortable with. If there is any unease at all with one another, it is better not to go ahead.

Wear a 15 eyed Dzi for good business and opportunity luck.

LOVE & RELATIONSHIPS – *Don't Hold Back*
There is love in the air for the Sheep person this month. Don't hold back on your emotions. If there is something you need to say to your partner, do not be afraid to share. You will not come across silly, gawky or love struck. Anything romantic you have to say will be taken just the way you meant it.

If you're already in a relationship, this is a good time to reconnect with your partner to revive some of the forgotten romance of your early days together. There's something special in the air for you this month, so don't miss out by being nonchalant in the romance department. Don't let commitments at work stop you from enjoying what promises to be a great month in terms of romance.

EDUCATION – *Success Indicated*
For the Sheep focusing on studies, this is an excellent month. Unlike mixed luck elsewhere, things are generally only positive for those focused on scholastic pursuits. Knowledge accumulation is prolific and new ideas sink in quickly. Make the best of the month by putting in the effort to match. You may surprise yourself with what you can achieve. Those hoping to earn accolades can achieve success. You catch the eye of the right people. Have firm goals in your mind and attaining them shouldn't be too difficult.

11TH MONTH
Dec 7th - Jan 5th 2011

YOU COULD GET ROBBED THIS MONTH

This month the Five Yellow of the year combines with the monthly violent star to bring threats to your physical safety. There is also loss indicated, mainly of money and material belongings. You face the danger of burglary and getting robbed, so be more alert this month. Carry a **blue rhino and elephant charm**, and make sure you have a set near the entrance to your home. Be extra careful about security this month. Check things yourself. You can't be too careful. You also risk being betrayed by people you thought you could trust. Not a good time to go into partnership or joint venture. Lay low when your luck is afflicted like this.

WORK & CAREER – *Keep Your Chin Up*

Although things may be tough at work, you need to keep your chin up. A dreary attitude could put you in a downward spiral and lower the opinions that others have of you. Things may not go quite as planned and you may a mishap or two. If you make mistakes, immediately take steps to correct yourself rather than look for excuses or someone else to put the blame on. Trying to cover your tracks will only make you look incompetent and deceitful. But genuine remorse and instant reaction to correct your mistake will be viewed on very favorably.

BUSINESS – *Money Disputes*
Trust your own judgment when it comes to making decisions. Although you may be used to consulting with others before proceeding ahead, this month your own decisions will probably be the best ones, not just for yourself but for everyone involved. There may be disputes when it comes to money matters between business partners. But before you jump to any conclusions, make sure you've investigated thoroughly before making accusations. Don't fall for third party troublemakers trying to come in between you and a business partner. Having said that, watch your back because you are in danger of being betrayed by those you trust.

LOVE & RELATIONSHIPS – *Not In The Mood*
Challenges at work may be weighing down on your mind, making you edgy and difficult to be around. This could have a negative impact on your relationships with those nearest and dearest to you. Try not to put everybody else in a foul mood just because you're down. Instead, let them cheer you up.

Try to be optimistic and you'll find yourself getting along with others much better. If you find yourself losing your cool over little things, stop yourself. Instead, get whatever is bothering you off your chest and you'll find yourself feeling much better.

This month is dry when it comes to romance, mainly because of your mood and how you're feeling. But don't sulk on your own. Get out, mix, date, socialize. The Sheep is a herd animal by instinct and just being around others with a more positive outlook than yourself can make the difference between a miserable month and one that promises to be quite enjoyable indeed.

HOME & PERSONAL SAFETY – *Afflicted*

You are afflicted by the burglary star this month, so it is a good idea to step up security in your home. Make sure the doors are locked each night and consider installing an alarm system. Take extra precautions with safety and teach your children rules about not talking to strangers or letting strangers in. Keep an **elephant and rhinoceros** near your front door as well as other doors that you feel are vulnerable to a break-in.

12TH MONTH
Jan 6th - Feb 3rd 2011

LUCK FROM HEAVEN
Your luck finally begins to change. As you near the end of the Tiger Year and begin to move towards the new Rabbit Year, plenty of new opportunities present themselves. Obstacles start to clear as if by magic and problems that were weighing you down miraculously get lifted. Helpful people show up in your life giving you the support you need, whether financially or otherwise.

Your energy levels improve, making you more energetic. This is a month when you can stop focusing on things that seem to be going wrong around you, and instead look to the future with hopeful anticipation. Things are looking up. Something changes in your life to bring excitement and passion back into the equation. Enjoy this month which promises to be better than the months preceding.

WORK & CAREER — *Be Proactive*
Take charge of things and be proactive. Don't wait till someone hands you a task. Sometimes your superiors

and bosses don't have the time to mollycoddle you, and the promotion will by default go to the employee with the most self-starting attitude.

Be proactive about earning that promotion, because luck is with you. Don't get greedy about the money and perks; be happy with what you get but till you get it, show what you're really worth. There is a lot to be accomplished this period, so start taking advantage of your situation. Share your good ideas, but present them in a manner that's impressive. Prepare yourself well for your presentations. Become indispensable.

BUSINESS – Be Prepared

Although you may have a pre-determined path that your business is heading down, something could crop up to make you change your mind. But the difficult thing may be to change your partners' minds as they may not agree with you! You may be emotionally torn up between going with your own instincts and listening to what everyone else is saying.

If you are sure about your findings, spend time preparing your case before putting it forward. You will never succeed in convincing anyone of anything if you don't present yourself in a prepared and logical manner. Don't take the easy way out just going with the flow. If you truly believe in what you are putting forward and are willing to spend the effort to support your case, others will come round to your way of thinking.

HOME & FAMILY – *A Social Time*

You're in the mood for family gatherings this month, and socializing this way has never been more fun! You may want to invite some outside friends to these get-togethers, especially if you have a small family. If there are many children involved it will be even nicer. For newly married Sheep, you may start feeling broody this month. This is an auspicious month for the Sheep wanting to start or expand a family.

LOVE & RELATIONSHIPS – *Heaven Luck!*

Your love life goes swell this month! How serious you want things to become with whoever you are currently dating is completely up to you! You enjoy the control you feel you have in any relationship, and if you've found a person with whom you have good chemistry with and who is willing to listen to your excited story-telling and ramblings, you could well be headed to the altar sooner than you think! The energies from the heavens are shining down on you, so enjoy this wonderful month!

Part 4
Updating House Feng Shui

It is so important to maintain the good feng shui of your home and protect yourself from the feng shui afflictions of the year.

For this reason as well as to ensure a smooth transition into the New Year, those born in the Sheep year should take careful note of time dimension feng shui especially in 2010, because the coming year can be quite precarious in terms of feng shui afflictions.

For this reason updating feng shui remedies and cures are exceptionally important for the Sheep! This means taking some important measures necessary to ensure the New Year brings both protection and good fortune.

You will need to make changes to the placement of decorative objects, undertake alterations to the way furniture is arranged in the public areas of your home and also make some adjustments to room usage. You should also take careful note of the amulets needed to ward off misfortune vibes flying into the Sheep location of your home.

Making changes to accommodate the annual chi energy patterns is needed to maintain a balance of good energy in the home. This is what will ensure a better year, as you are then protected against getting hit by nasty surprises and misfortune happenings.

This is something not many people are aware of, as a result of which even when a home has been very well designed according to feng shui principles, when no effort is made to accommodate yearly changes of energy, sometimes bad luck descends unexpectedly causing sudden problems to descend on the family.

Usually, misfortune brought by afflictive flying stars can be severe, serious enough to cause a high degree of stress and tribulations. In fact, when unlucky energy inadvertently flies into the part of your home where your **main door** is located, or where your

PART 4 - UPDATING HOUSE FENG SHUI

bedroom is sited, you, and often your family, risk being hit by some misfortune luck. This is true even when your personal horoscope chart shows your luck is good for the year.

Misfortune can manifest as a sudden illness, an unexpected accident or loss, a court case or a significant reversal of fortune that brings hardship. It is advisable then to anticipate this kind of problem, address it and then install remedies and cures. This is the best way to practice feng shui with great effectiveness.

> The location and severity of feng shui afflictions that bring bad luck to residents in any building are revealed by annual flying stars. These are numbers that move around a specially constructed feng shui chart based on an ancient formula that maps out the changing chi movements of each New Year.

These changes alter the luck patterns of all buildings every New Year. Attending to it is part of the time aspects of feng shui practice. It is something that should be incorporated into an annual renewal of chi program for the home. Attending to this renewal process ensures that the energy of your abodes stay fresh and vigorous.

Yearly Feng Shui Afflictions

These bring negative luck, causing misfortune, accidents, loss and a variety of ills to manifest. This part of the book explains the severity and location of the different afflictions in the Year of the Tiger and highlights those of particular importance to those born in the year of the Sheep. Once you know what and where the afflictions are, it is not difficult to deal with them using element cures and other powerful traditional feng shui methods.

It is important to subdue annual feng shui afflictions because these have the potential to create havoc in your life. Misfortune can come in a variety of ways. Sometimes they manifest as severe illness suffered by some member of the family; or they can cause loss of wealth, loss of good name or loss of a loved one.

It is not difficult to control feng shui afflictions and doing so helps prevent bad luck from occurring, so everyone should really take the trouble to do so. It is worthwhile making the effort, because for most part, the remedies involve little effort.

In the past, this aspect of feng shui was simply ignored by modern day practitioners, leaving many vulnerable to reversals of fortune although in recent years, awareness of time dimension feng shui has

PART 4 - UPDATING HOUSE FENG SHUI

increased substantially. Master practitioners of feng shui in Asia and around the world, now go to great lengths to study, analyze and deal with time related feng shui afflictions at the start of each New Year.

> The cut off date when energy patterns change, occur around February 4th, which is regarded as the first day of Spring – in Chinese known as the *lap chun*. This is not to be confused with the lunar New Year date which is determined by the Chinese lunar calendar. The Chinese use their solar calendar (known as the *Hsia Calendar*) to track feng shui energy changes. The monthly change of energy patterns in Part 3 of the book, for instance, uses the Hsia calendar to determine the dates when each month starts.

The feng shui chart of any year is usually depicted in a 9 x 9 sector Lo Shu square with a number in each grid. These numbers are determined by the ruling or center number which in 2010 is 8. Once the center number is known, the rest of the numbers in the different grids of the Lo Shu square can be determined. The numbers 1 through 9 in each of the nine grids of the Lo Shu Square offer insights into the way the pattern of luck has moved in any built up structure or building. This investigation precedes the updating of feng shui.

2010 Annual Feng Shui chart

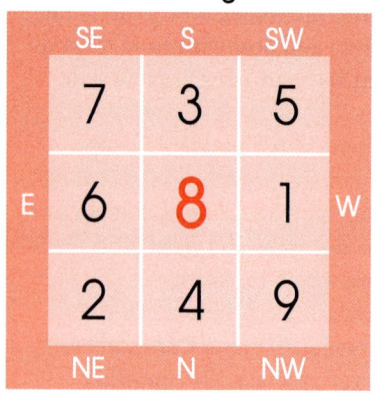

SE	S	SW
7	3	5
6	**8**	1
2	4	9
NE	N	NW

(E on left, W on right)

The numbers in this chart change or "fly" from year to year, reflecting changes in energy in the different direction sectors. Each of the numbers in the different compass locations reveal the quality of energy ruling that location in 2010.

The chart also reveals the good luck sectors – i.e. those parts of your house that enjoy the most auspicious luck during the year. If the lucky numbers fly into the sector that houses your main door or bedroom, or into any part of the home where you spend a considerable amount of time, then the good energy of that location showers you with good fortune. Sometimes the feng shui of your bedroom can be so good that it can override any kind of low energy you may be suffering from in your horoscope chart for the year.

When auspicious numbers enter into the location of your animal sign, it will benefit you for that year.

Hence understanding the annual chart feng shui enables you to subdue bad luck and bad feng shui; and to enhance good luck and good feng shui.

> **When feng shui afflictions of your living and work spaces are treated with feng shui cures, and the lucky sectors are activated with auspicious decorative objects or celestial creatures, your luck for the year is sure to instantly improve.**

You can overcome obstacles to success more effectively, and make better decisions by tracking your luck through each month of the year. Timing plays a crucial role in the success factor and when armed with prior knowledge of good and bad months, you are certain to have a positive competitive edge.

Updating your feng shui brings powerful benefits as you will know exactly how to be protected against sudden/major changes of fortunes. Those unprotected are vulnerable not only to annual afflictions but also to monthly ill winds that might be blowing your way. It is so important then to know about good and bad months.

Misfortune usually comes suddenly, descending on you when least expected. It can come as illness, or manifest as court action, or worse, as some kind of personal loss. Misfortune can hit at anytime. Don't think that bad things do not happen to good people, because they do. Since it requires so little effort to guard against bad luck and bad feng shui, it seems foolish not to do so.

Luck of Different Parts of the Home

The annual feng shui chart reveals the luck of every part of the house, categorized into compass sectors. So every corner of the home must be investigated. Each sector has a number from 1 through 9, and there are eight outer sectors plus the center. In 2010 the center sector ruling number is 8. The remaining numbers are identified once the center number is known.

These numbers enable a knowledgeable feng shui practitioner to instantly identify afflicted sectors. These are the parts of the house where remedies need to be put in place to suppress the afflictions. Doing so – subduing the afflictions of the different parts of the house – brings protection to the whole house!

In the same way the luckiest sectors can also be ascertained and then activated to manifest good luck. When individual sectors get enhanced, the improved

PART 4 - UPDATING HOUSE FENG SHUI

chi energy spreads to the rest of the house. It is vital to study the feng shui chart for 2010 which is done in this book. Then you, the reader can superimpose it onto the layout sketches of your home. You should use a good compass to identify the compass locations of your home.

> Familiarize yourself with the chart of 2010 and systematically list down the afflictions that are particularly harmful for your house. Remember that when bad luck numbers occur in rooms that you or your family use, that is when placing the correct remedies and cures takes on some urgency.

When these bad luck numbers come into your bedroom, or afflict important doors and areas of the home (such as the dining area and family area) then once again remedies become very important.

The same analogy applies to good luck stars. When these fly into important and heavy traffic rooms, the auspicious luck gets activated, and they then bring benefits to residents; and when they enter into small rooms like store rooms or tight little alcoves in the home, their good effect does not benefit the household as much.

Activating Good Star Numbers

You need to remember that in flying star feng shui, good and bad luck numbers need to be activated either by placing an object that symbolizes a producing element (such as Water element producing Wood element in a Wood sector like East or SE) or with an auspicious decorative item. Here, knowing what **celestial creature** to display and what **element** is favorable for the year will help you to vastly improve your feng shui.

Other ways to activate good numbers is to increase the level of yang energy in the corners benefiting from the year's good fortune numbers. Thus using bright lights and increasing sound levels in the center of the house in 2010, for example, should benefit the household greatly.

This is because the center plays host to the auspicious 8 and activating it is sure to bring benefits. In 2010, the center of the house should be energized by the presence of **multiple crystal balls** – eight should be an excellent number. This strengthens the Earth element of the center and since

8 is itself an Earth element number, and considering that the earth element symbolizes wealth in 2010, enhancing Earth energy is excellent indeed.

In fact, crystal balls of any kind will be very beneficial for the center of the home in 2010. The large **Tara Crystal Ball** which we brought out last year to energize 8 in the SE sector then was a great success for many people and for those who want to use these again in 2010, just move it to the center of the room. Make sure you twirl it daily because this activates the positive effects of crystal ball; as the ball contains the praises to the Goddess Tara, twirling the ball activates its wish-fulfilling aspect.

There is also another crystal ball which contains the powerful six syllable *Om Mani Padme Hum* mantra in Tibetan. For those wanting to create an aura of blessings in the home you can also place this **Om Mani Crystal Ball** in the center of the home, or on the coffee table in the living room. A golden 8 embedded inside the crystal ball activates the power of 8. To make the feng shui even more effective, make sure you keep the light turned on as much as possible in the center of the home as fire enhances earth. Light combined with the action of twirling the ball ensures that good positive yang energy gets generated. This draws auspicious energy into the home.

We have also designed a beautiful **Crystal 8** with real gold flakes embedded within to be placed in the center of the home. This will add significantly to the enhancement of the Earth element which will be so beneficial in 2010. Another powerful enhancer which can be placed in the center of the home to activate the auspicious 8 is the **Victory Banner Windchime**.

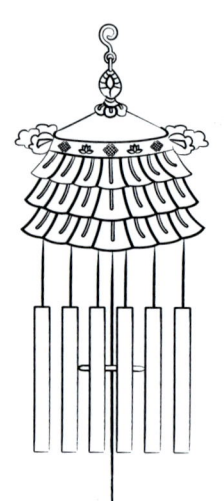

Place the Victory Banner Windchime in the center of the house to activate the lucky 8.

PART 4 - UPDATING HOUSE FENG SHUI

Feng Shui Chart of 2010

The feng shui chart of 2010 is created by placing the ruling number of the year in the center. We have already taken note that the ruling number of the year is 8, and considering that we are currently in the period of 8, this makes the number 8 extremely significant and very lucky indeed this year.

2010 Year of the Golden Tiger

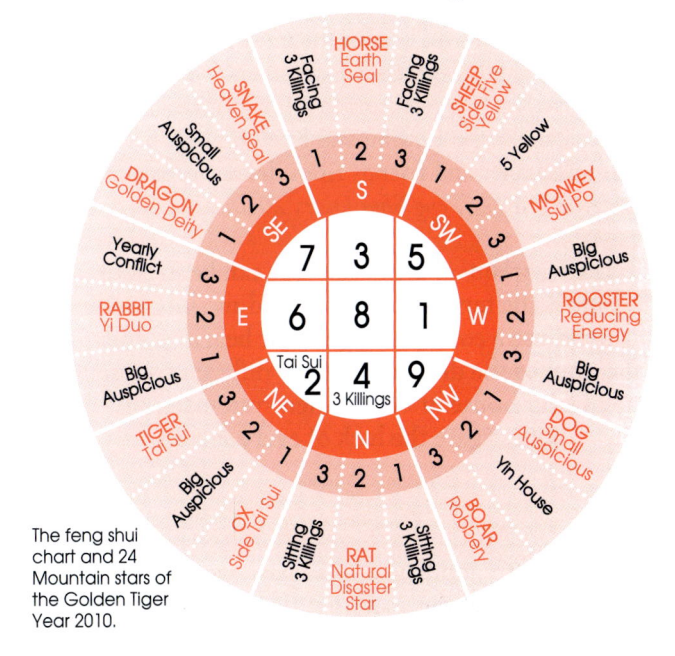

The feng shui chart and 24 Mountain stars of the Golden Tiger Year 2010.

Activating the 8 in the center brings amazing good fortune and this is the reason why we are strongly recommending the **crystal 8 with gold** for the center of the house! Those whose Kua number or Lo Shu number is 8 can expect the year to go well for them, as this is also the period of 8.

Crystal 8 with gold specks embedded inside - for the center of the living room.

Just make sure you make an effort to activate the 8 in the center of the house. Those whose Kua number is 8 will benefit the most and this also includes women whose Kua is 5. This is because Kua 5 transforms to 8 for women. You can check the Lo Shu and Kua numbers of your loved ones and friends from the resource tables contained in our *Feng Shui Diary 2010*.

> **The feng shui chart of the year can be used to study the feng shui of any building, but you must use a compass to get your bearings and to anchor the directions of the different rooms of your house or office. Then systematically investigate the luck of every sector.**

Luck Stars of the 24 Mountains

In addition to numbers of the chart, we also study the influences of the stars that fly into the 24 mountain directions of the compass. These "stars" do not carry the same weighting in terms of their strength and luck-bringing potential, but they add important nuances to annual chart readings, and are extracted from the Almanac. Incorporating the influence of the stars adds depth to a reading of the year's feng shui energy, and for each of the twelve signs.

Together, the stars and the numbers reveal accurate and significant things about the year, and when we add the influence of the year's elements, readings for each of the animal signs become very potent and exciting. This assists you to get the best from the year. The seamless merging of Chinese Zodiac Astrology with feng shui comprise the core strength and great value of our little astrology books which we take great joy and pride in researching and writing every year.

This is the seventh year of our *Fortune & Feng Shui* list. Each year we delve a little deeper into all that influences the fortune and luck of the twelve animal signs, and the feng shui recommendations contained herein take account of these influences. Please use the analysis in this section to move from sector to sector and from room to room in your home, systematically installing feng shui remedies affected by bad chi energy. Place powerful decorative energizers and protective images to create and safeguard good luck.

ILLNESS STAR 2
Hits the Northeast in 2010

SE	S	SW
7	3	5
6 (E)	8	1 (W)
2	4	9
NE	N	NW

This is the Illness Star which flies to NE in 2010. The "star" brings propensity to getting sick for those whose bedroom or door is located in the NE sector of the home.

The illness star 2 flies to the NE in 2010. This is an Earth element sector and since the illness star 2 is an Earth element number, it makes the illness affliction extremely strong in the Year of the Tiger. Earth flying into Earth suggests that those residing in the NE of their homes, or having an office or a front door in the NE tend to be vulnerable to getting sick. Unless the illness bringing energy in

Cures for the Illness Star of 2010

There are excellent remedies that can be used to suppress the illness star. In 2010, a **Tiger/Dragon Wu Lou** would be especially effective. Another excellent cure is the powerful **Antahkarana Symbol** which is powerful enough to suppress the strong illness star this year, especially when it is made of metal. Brass is especially good as metal exhausts the Earth energy of the illness star.

The symbol itself is a powerful symbol of healing and has a three dimensional effect that cuts directly into harmful negative energy. Get this symbol and place under the bed if your bed is located in the NE of your bedroom, or if your bedroom itself is in the NE. Sleep with the symbol of the Antahkarana under your pillow, or better yet, wear the Antahkarana ring preferably made in yellow gold. The energies emitted by the powerful Antakarana symbol – a trinity of 7 placed inside a circle - will effectively keep sickness at bay.

The healing symbol of Antahkarana.

this part of buildings – homes and offices – **gets strongly suppressed,** people residing or working in that part of the building are likely to develop physical ailments. And since the illness star is strong this year, it is harder to control.

If your bedroom is located in the NE sector of your house, you must make sure that suitable remedies are placed in your bedroom to suppress illness vibes.

When the main door of the house is located in the NE, the constant opening and closing of the door is sure to activate the illness bringing star. It is advisable to try and use another door located in another sector. If this is not possible then try exhausting the Earth energy here.

Remove all Earth element items such as crystals, porcelain vases or stone objects. Also keep lights here dim to reduce Fire element energy. This is because Fire element strengthens Earth element.

LITIGATION STAR 3
Hits the South in 2010

SE	S	SW
7	**3**	5
6	8	1
2	4	9
NE	N	NW

This is the unlucky 3 Star which brings court case & quarrels. It flies to the South in 2010, affecting all of you whose room or office are located in the South. Use red or Fire energy to suppress.

The noisy, quarrelsome star 3, which brings the aggravating energy of litigation and court cases, flies to the South part of homes and offices in 2010. This star brings an air of hostility and creates a variety of problems associated with arguments, fights and misunderstandings to everyone directly hit by it. In extreme cases, when this Wood element star is enhanced, the quarrelling can lead to court cases and even violence for residents spending time in the South. The number 3 star can cause a host of interpersonal strife to flare up even between the closest of allies, friends and loved ones. It causes tempers to fray and usually manifests in a great deal of impatience.

Fortunately for anyone with a bedroom in the South, the quarrelsome star 3 is less strong this year because its intrinsic Wood element is exhausted by the Fire energy of the South. The 3 Star is a Wood element star and the traditional way of overcoming this is to exhaust it with Fire element energy. Anything that suggests Fire is an excellent cure, so all kinds of lights and the color red are suitable remedies. Hence because the South is so strongly associated with fire energy, the sector itself has its own in-built remedy!

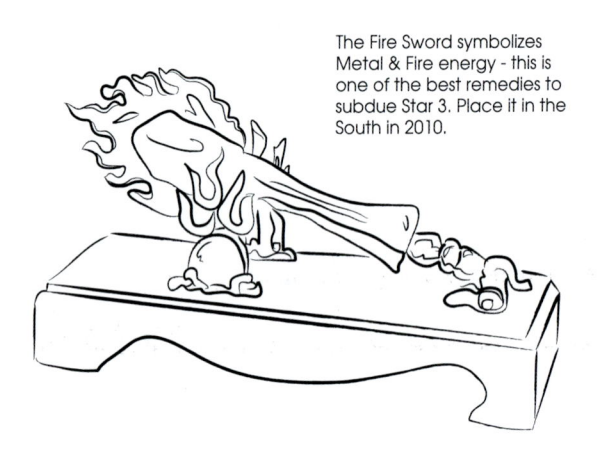

The Fire Sword symbolizes Metal & Fire energy - this is one of the best remedies to subdue Star 3. Place it in the South in 2010.

Earth Seal in the South

A good indication for the South location in 2010 is that the sector benefits from the presence of the **Earth Seal** brought by the luck star of the 24 mountains; this brings good fortune to those residing in this part of the house, especially if you take action to enhance this energy with Earth element activators such as **solid crystal** or **glass globes**.

Houses that face South should place the **Fire Sword** here as a safeguard against being hauled into court or getting involved in a tiresome legal battle perhaps left over from past years. Should you be already involved in litigation, or find yourself in a prolonged battle with someone or some company, the number 3 star will hurt you if you have a bedroom in the South or if your house is facing South. If this is the case with you, do use **strong bright lights** to help you overcome it. A dramatic remedy which brings some relief from aggravation is simply to paint the South part of the house **a bright red** – perhaps a wall or a door if this is the front part of the home.

MISFORTUNE STAR 5
Hits the Southwest in 2010

SE	S	SW
7	3	5
6	8	1
2	4	9
NE	N	NW

(E on left, W on right)

The Five Yellow Star *Wu Wang*, flies to the SW hunting the matriarchal energy of every home. This is a serious affliction which must be suppressed with the 5 element pagoda with "Hum" empowering syllable.

The Five Yellow star, also known as the *wu wang* flies to the SW in 2010 making it a very serious affliction this year. This is a star to be feared as it brings aggravations, misfortunes and most of all in 2010, a big weakness to the Matriarch of the family.

This is because SW is usually associated with the mother energy of any home, and in feng shui, when the matriarchal energy gets afflicted, it usually has a strong impact on the rest of the family as well. This is because SW is the source of the family's nurturing chi. As we are currently in the period of 8, the SW/NE directional axis exerts a great deal of

PART 4 - UPDATING HOUSE FENG SHUI

strong chi for any home and when the energy of this axis brings misfortune, it must be firmly subdued. In 2010 this axis direction appears to be powerfully afflicted, with five yellow (*wu wang*) in the SW and 2 in the NE.

The *wu wang* is very dangerous in normal years, but in 2010, it is extremely strong as it is an earth star flying into an earth sector. Likewise, the illness star 2 in the NE is also strong! The *wu wang* thus gets strengthened, as a result of which, it can create havoc for mothers and also for other older women of the household. Those having their bedroom here will also feel its negative impact and when a house faces SW, the *wu wang* can bring misfortunes that affect the entire household of residents. If there is a door in the SW that you frequently use, the *wu wang* gets activated, and this further compounds its strength. So, it is advisable to use another door if possible. The opening and closing of doors activates the energy around it.

Everyone must definitely suppress the pernicious effects of this number 5 star – otherwise its negative influence can spread to other parts of the house. It must be strongly curbed with powerful metallic and symbolic remedies. These should best be prominently placed, on a table or sideboard in the

SW of the house and office as well as in the SW of afflicted bedrooms and living rooms.

> ## Cures for the Wu Wang
> For 2010, we recommend 3 powerful cures for this affliction. These should be used together for fast and powerful results. The remedies are:
>
> ### 1) Five Element Pagoda with Ten Powerful Mantras
> This year, this traditional remedy comes with a larger base and the powerful mantras are stamped all round the base of the pagoda. This version of the 5 element pagoda is recommended for use in larger rooms and is best when placed above ground, preferably on a table. The mantras on the pagoda transform it into a powerful object which should be respected, so place it on a table.
>
> The Five Element Pagoda with Ten Powerful Mantras is recommended for larger rooms afflicted by the *wu wang* star.

2) The Five Element Big Bell

This cure is best when 12 inches high. The bell is divided into 5 horizontal sections, each one signifying the 5 elements. The bell also has powerful mantras embossed on its outside. The remedy comes from striking of the bell. Here, the sound of metal struck on metal is what will suppress the negative influences of the five yellow. Strike the bell at least once a day and more often if residents are going through a hard time. The sound of the bell with the resonance of the mantras is very powerful for dispelling bad vibes. All misfortune luck gets alleviated instantly. This is the most powerful cure against the Five Yellow. If you prefer, you can use the ringing bell instead and the way to suppress the *wu wang* is to ring this bell each day.

3) Double Circle Pendant

If you want to ensure continuous suppression of any ongoing misfortune luck or if you are going through really tough times associated with broken relationships and loss of income (such as losing your job) it is beneficial for members of the family to wear the Double Circle pendant. This will activate powerful metal energy to exhaust the effects of the *wu wang*. Better yet if the pendant has multiple circles and in the center there is a square design. This indicates the *wu wang* is kept under control.

Please note that unless suppressed, the *wu wang* brings severe illness, accidents and loss that occur in many aspects of life. It is the catalyst for bringing all kinds of misfortunes. It can cause your life to suddenly collapse around you without warning.

When you read about tragedies striking a family, you can be sure that the Five Yellow is somehow responsible, either because it afflicts the main door or the room the person occupies. Sometimes, just facing the *wu wang* direction can bring some kind of bad luck.

If your main door, your bedroom or even your office desk is afflicted by the *wu wang*, the affliction must be dealt with before the 4th February 2010. Do not be careless or forget about it as bad luck can manifest quickly. When it does it might be too late to do something about it. Prevention is better than cure, so do not wait until it is too late.

Those living in SW-facing houses should take note of the months when you need to be extra careful of the Five Yellow. We stress this because it is a serious feng shui affliction in 2010.

PART 4 - UPDATING HOUSE FENG SHUI

> As a person born in the Sheep year you must be extra careful in the month of May as this is the month when the *wu wang* flies into your month chart. This is when you are subjected to a truly double whammy of bad luck so do be careful. You must get out of the SW in this month!

Misfortunes caused by the Five Yellow in 2010 can be severe business loss or threatening terminal illness. Houses that face the SW require one or all three of the remedies suggested. This is because houses that face SW are sitting NE which is being hit by the illness star. Metal energy works well here at both the front and back of the house.

> If you reside in a room located in the SW, your cure should be inside your room. Make sure that the cures are in place from February 4th, the start of the Chinese solar year.

While remedies used in previous years can be recycled after they have been cleansed with salt, it is better to retire them by throwing them into the sea or a fast moving river. It is always better to use new products with fresh new energy. New remedies are better for suppressing feng shui afflictions, as the energy of new objects are more vigorous and thus more effective.

Sheep people belong to the Earth element, so the *wu wang's* Earth element brings **competitive pressures** into their life. This is one of the effects of the *wu wang* on the Sheep - more people tend to want to compete with you or manifest **envy and jealousy.** Also, in 2010, the element of Earth stands for wealth luck that is in danger of declining in value due to the lack of Water during the year. To be safeguarded from these two kinds of misfortunes, Sheep must remedy its exposure to this powerful misfortune star.

Observe the "NO RENOVATION RULE" for the Southwest in 2010

It is extremely harmful if you were to undertake any kind of knocking, banging or digging in the SW in 2010. This will especially hurt the mother of the household. So do observe the "No Renovation" rule for the SW during 2010. Any kind of demolition work poses serious danger. Misfortunes are sure to manifest. It is especially dangerous to drill floors, knock down walls, dig holes in the ground, engage in any kind of destructive work or make excessive banging kind of noise. Any of these activities have the effect of activating the *wu wang* which is sure to trigger

PART 4 - UPDATING HOUSE FENG SHUI

very severe misfortune luck to suddenly manifest. The way to safeguard against this is to keep the SW location of the home very quiet in 2010. If you really have to undertake renovations in your house and it encroaches into the SW sector, make sure your cures are in place **and** make very sure the renovation does not start or end in the SW.

No one should be staying in the SW sector when renovations are going on. If you are adding to the SW however, and not disturbing the space with banging and digging, then that kind of renovation is acceptable; and can even be auspicious. But as long as you are demolishing or digging the earth/floor, it is advisable to postpone whatever you may be planning for the sector.

Do not start or end renovations in the SW sector in 2010. Better yet if you can avoid renovating, digging or disturbing the SW completely.

ROBBERY STAR 7
Strikes the Southeast in 2010

SE	S	SW
7	3	5
6	8	1
2	4	9
NE	N	NW

(E on left, W on right)

The Robbery Star also brings violence & turmoil in your life. At its worst, the 7 brings armed robbery that can cause fatal results. Protect against it with the Blue Rhino & Elephant.

This is a very unwelcome affliction that is brought by the number 7. It is a number that causes political turmoil and sparks aggressive behavior that can become something serious very fast and this is because it is the violent star. It brings out the worst in all who come under its influence or is afflicted by it.

In 2010, it flies to the SE where its presence creates dangerous situations for those residing here in the SE sector. This star number completely dominates the sector because being of the Metal element, it easily controls the Wood Element of the SE. So the 7 is very lethal here.

The SE is the place of the eldest daughter, so daughters should be especially careful. Anyone living in the SE should also be very careful as this star number brings danger of violence and burglary. It is advisable to try and avoid this sector.

For 2010, because the water element is so lacking during the year, the best remedy for the SE – for the whole house to be protected from the 7 star, residents should display the special **Blue Rhino and Elephant water globe**. This will be a very powerful cure for the violent burglary star. Placing or incorporating the water globe or water motif here is also an excellent idea.

The good news is that in the year 2010 the luck Stars of the 24 mountains for the SE are extremely auspicious. Thus the *Star of the Golden Deity* which brings heaven's blessings benefits all those residing in the SE1 location. At the same time the SE3 location is favored by the *Heavenly Seal* which also brings auspicious energy. This benefits anyone staying here.

These two powerful heavenly stars of the 24 mountains are an excellent buffer against the annoyance of the burglary star as it is sandwiched between two powerful stars. This helps residents of the SW overcome burglary woes in 2010. Remember that the best way to overcome the negative effect of 7 is to have a large water feature as Water exhausts the vitality of 7.

Water is always auspicious for the SE where it strengthens the intrinsic Wood energy here. Those who already have a water feature here such as a pond in the garden or an internal water feature in the living room will be happy to know that in addition to generating good fortune luck for the eldest daughter of the family, water here suppress the burglary star of 2010 AND brings much needed Water energy for the year.

The Tai Sui Resides in the Northeast in 2010

The 2010 *Tai Sui* resides in the location of NE3 which is the home location of the Crouching Tiger; however, despite occupying the den of the Tiger, this year's Tai Sui is not wrathful, and like the Tai Sui of the previous year is not given to quick anger even when disturbed or confronted. Nevertheless, to be on the safe side, it is advisable to keep the Tai Sui appeased and happy. The best way of doing this is to place the Tai Sui plaque with a **specially written Taoist talisman**. This not only appeases the Tai Sui, it also successfully enlists the Tai Sui's help to attract prosperity and abundance.

PART 4 - UPDATING HOUSE FENG SHUI

> NOTE: An important reminder for 2010 is to not disturb the place of the Tai Sui which means the NE3 location should not be renovated this year. Refrain from drilling, digging, banging and knocking down walls or digging holes in the ground. Those starting renovations in 2010 to change to a Period 8 house are advised not to start or end their renovations in NE3 and to avoid starting or ending their renovations in November when the direction of the Tai Sui is afflicted by misfortune star of *wu wang*.

The Tai Sui is in a side conflict with those born in the year of the Sheep and because the Sheep is also afflicted by the *wu wang*, the Tai Sui confrontation brings some serious problems.

The Effect of the Tai Sui Affliction

If you believe in feng shui, do take the affliction of the Tai Sui seriously. This is emphasized in the Treatise on Harmonizing Times and Distinguishing Directions compiled under the patronage of the Qianlong Emperor during his reign in the mid Eighteenth century. The Emperor placed great importance on the astrological influences on the luck of the dynasty.

He particularly stressed on correct ways for selecting times and aligning houses and in fact went to great lengths to ensure that all knowledge on these matters were properly catalogued for posterity. The Treatise confirms that the astrology of the Tai Sui has been recognized since mid-century BCE (for over 2000 years) and it states that the locations where the Tai Sui resides and where the Tai Sui has just vacated are lucky locations.

So note that in 2010, the locations of NE1 and NE3 are lucky. Those having their rooms in these two locations will enjoy the patronage and protection of the Tai Sui in 2010.

The Treatise explains that it is unlucky to reside in the location where the Tai Sui is progressing towards i.e. clockwise on the astrology compass and in 2010 this means the East 2 location; it is unlucky to directly confront the Tai Sui's residence. It is unlucky to "face" the Tai Sui because this is deemed rude, so the advice for 2010 is not to directly face NE3 direction. Actually, doing so also causes you to directly confront the Tiger, and this is definitely not advisable. So for 2010 you must remember not to face NE3 even if this is your most favored direction under the Eight Mansions School of feng shui. When you face the Tai Sui, nothing you do will go smoothly as obstacles surface unexpectedly and friends turn into adversaries.

It is very beneficial to place the beautiful **Pi Yao** in the NE as this celestial chimera is incredibly auspicious. For getting on the good side of the Tai Sui, they are also effective. They bring exceptional good fortune into the home. Get them in jade or any Earth color to enhance their power in a year when Wood chi brings wealth and Earth chi brings productive resources.

Place a Pi Yao in the NE sector of the home and office in 2010 to get on the good side of the Tai Sui.

The Three Killings Flies to the North in 2010

In 2010 the North of every building is afflicted by the Three Killings. This feng shui aggravation affects only the primary directions, but that means its bad effects are felt over a larger area of the house – 90 degrees! This affliction brings three severe misfortunes associated with loss, grief and sadness.

Its location each year is charted according to the animal sign that rules the year. Thus it flies to the North in 2010 because the Tiger belongs to the Triangle of Affinity made up of the Tiger, Dog and Horse and of these three animal signs, it is the Horse which occupies a cardinal direction (South).

> **The Three Killings is in the North this year, the direction that is directly opposite the Horse.**

The Three Killings cause three kinds of loss, the loss of one's good reputation, the loss of a loved one and the loss of wealth. When you suffer a sudden reversal of fortune, it is usually due to being hit by the three killings. In 2010, the three killings reside in the North where it poses some danger to the middle sons of the family. Anyone occupying the North are very vulnerable to being hit by the Three Killings.

Cures for the Three Killings

In terms of cures, we are recommending the three divine guardians - comprising the Chi Lin, the Fu Dog and the Pi Yao.

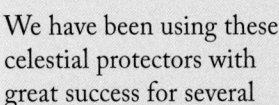

The Three Divine Guardians can be used to control the Three Killings affliction in the North in 2010.

We have been using these celestial protectors with great success for several years now and we can continue using them for 2010. It is however advisable to bring in newly minted ones to ensure their energy is fresh and there is strong vigor and vitality.

The three guardians are a great favorite with the Chinese and they create a powerful and invisible shield of protective energy that prevents the Three Killings from passing into the home or office.

It is a good idea to keep all North sector doors and windows closed during the afternoon hours as this is an effective way of preventing the energy of the Three Killings from entering.

Another powerful set of cures to overpower the three killings in the year of the Tiger are the **Three Deities** each sitting on a Tiger and therefore symbolizing their dominance over this powerful beast. Deities that sit on the Tiger are usually also wealth-bringing Gods.

The most effective then is to line up the Wealth God sitting on a Tiger (Tsai Shen Yeh), the Eight Immortal sitting on a Tiger and one of the 18 Arhats sitting on a Tiger. The symbolism of these three powerful Deities cannot be matched and their presence in the home is also an effective way of avoiding all the difficult luck brought by the Tiger in 2010.

A Wealth God sitting on a Tiger symbolizes his dominance over the animal and displaying his image in the home helps you bring the fierce energies of the Tiger Year under control.

THE LUCKY STAR 4 bringing
Romance & Study Luck to the North

SE	S	SW
7	3	5
6	8	1
2	4	9
NE	N	NW

(E on left, W on right)

Lucky Star 4 flies North bringin love & romance this part of houses in 2010. The star 4 is also beneficial for anyone engaged in writing, study and work.

The North comes out of a challenging year to play host to the romance-bringing star in 2010. Last year, the North had been afflicted by the *wu wang*, but this year this is the location which attracts love and marriage opportunities, developments of the heart brought by the peach blossom vibes here. This luck is considered good for singles and unmarried people but is viewed with suspicion for those who are already married. *Peach blossom luck* is usually linked to temptations of the heart and to unfaithful behavior for the older married. As such this is not a star favored by those already married. So if your room is in the North part of the house and you are already married it is not a bad idea to symbolically suppress it with **bright lights** or Fire element energy.

This should prevent either husband or wife succumbing to temptation coming their way. Placing an **amethyst geode tied with red string** and attached to the bed is a Taoist way of keeping the marriage stable, and spouses faithful.

> Unmarried people who want to activate their marriage luck can do so with the presence of all the marriage symbols such as the **dragon and phoenix,** and the **double happiness character**. Here in the North the romance star favors young men who are still single. So those of you keen on enhancing marriage luck should activate your peach blossom luck by placing a **bejeweled Rat** in the North. However do note that the Chinese usually do not favor romance blossoming in the year of the Tiger and they usually wait until the following year of the Rabbit before committing themselves in a new love relationship.
>
> The double happiness symbol is ideal for attracting marriage luck. It should be worn or incorporated into house or room decor for best results.

Scholastic Luck

Those residing in the North part of the house will also enjoy the other influences brought by the same number 4 star which are also related to scholastic and literary pursuits. The number 4's literary side is strong, bringing academic luck to those residing in this part of the home. Those facing North will also benefit from this powerful star of learning and is especially suitable for students and those sitting for examinations.

> The direction North stands for career luck so this auspicious number is a very positive star here. The only problem will be that love can also be a distraction, so if you want to enhance the scholastic side of this star, you should place literary symbols here.

The number 4 benefits those engaged in writing and literary careers. Those employed in a writing career or in the media or are involved in any kind of academic pursuits benefit from staying in the North. Enhancing this part of the house is sure to bring benefits.

Feng shui energizers for the North in 2010 are categorized into those benefiting the romance side and those wanting to activate the scholastic side. For love and romance, place **mandarin ducks** here and better yet, hang a **love mirror** to reflect in the energies of the cosmic universe from outside. Meanwhile those wanting to jump start their scholastic or literary pursuits should look for a good specimen of a **single-pointed quartz crystal** and then write a powerful wishfulfilling mantra on it. This is an excellent way of helping you to improve your concentration and your studies.

WHITE STAR 1 brings Triumphant Success to the West

SE	S	SW
7	3	5
6	8	1
2	4	9
NE	N	NW

(E on left, W on right)

The Victory Star is in the West - it is flanked by the 2 "Big Auspicious" stars of the 24 mountains. This makes the West sector extremely lucky in 2010 and those having rooms here can take advantage of this.

Those residing in rooms in the West corner of your house will benefit from the white star of victory, the number 1 star which brings triumph and success in 2010. This star number helps you to

PART 4 - UPDATING HOUSE FENG SHUI

win in any competitive situation. It is the star that brings triumphant luck helping anyone receiving its chi energy to emerge successfully in any kind of competition. The attainment of success is easier for you, especially if you also energize the number 1 star correctly and effectively.

In 2010, this star brings good fortune to young women, especially the youngest daughters of families and also the youngest women in any household. However, please note that the number 1 star in 2010 is not as vigorous as it was last year. There is definitely a relative reduction in energy. Anyone residing in this part of the house will benefit from wearing the **Victory Banner**. It is important that this be made of gold or metal to strengthen the Metal element of this star.

The Victory Banner is a symbol of winning over the competition. Excellent for those in the running for a promotion.

CELESTIAL STAR 6
Creates Windfall Luck in the East

SE	S	SW
7	3	5
6	8	1
2	4	9
NE	N	NW

E (left side), W (right side)

Celestial luck of 6 brings excellent news through the year. The number 6 stands for heavenly celestial energy which unites with Earth and mankind to create the trinity of Tien Ti Ren.

This is the number 6 white star which is associated with the powerful **Trigram Chien**, so its presence in the East creates the synergy luck between father and eldest son. When the bedroom of the family's eldest son is located in this sector of the house, he is certain to benefit very much from unexpected good fortune, the kind that comes without warning, and is thus a welcome surprise. The 6 star brings heaven's celestial blessings. There is also the presence of the *Golden Deity* star which strengthens the help from heaven diagnosis for the East. To activate this auspicious star, welcome in a **Golden Deity sitting on a Dragon** to this sector. One such deity is the White Dzambhala –

the Tibetan Deity of Wealth – which sits on a Dragon and carries a gem-spouting mongoose!

Inviting White Dzambala into the East sector of your home will enhance the auspicious Golden Deity Star of the 24 mountains.

In Flying Star feng shui interpretation the number 6 signifies everything to do with the management of economics and finances. At its peak 6 stands for authority, influence and control over money, like being the Head of the Federal Reserve Board. When 6 appears in the East it suggests economic power does well in the hands of a young man. This is also a Military star which brings promotions and mentor luck.

It is incredibly beneficial to activate this auspicious star to benefit the whole household and this can be done by displaying **6 large smooth coins** in the East sector. Doing so ensures that everything will move smoothly for the household. It is also a very powerful way of attracting Mentor Luck into the household – powerful and influential friends who can and will assist you, opening doorways to opportunities for you.

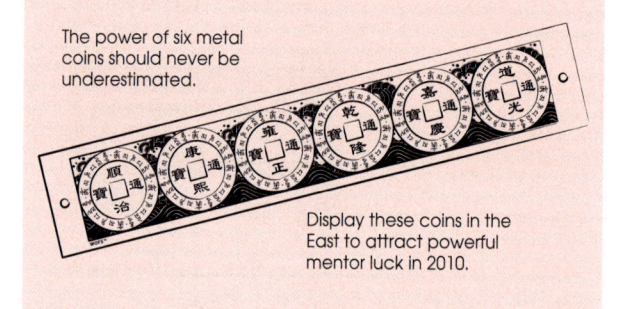

The power of six metal coins should never be underestimated.

Display these coins in the East to attract powerful mentor luck in 2010.

Updating Your Feng Shui

Updating feng shui is something that many wealthy and powerful families in places like Hong Kong, Taiwan and now China arrange for without fail each year. In recent years, the practice is also becoming increasingly popular in Singapore, Malaysia and Indonesia. Today, families consult feng shui retainers who use their expertise to insure homes against the intangible feng shui afflictions of the year. These days anyone keen to do so can update their feng shui. At *World of Feng Shui*, the annual feng shui chart is analyzed each year. This makes it possible for us to understand the nature and location of bad luck afflictions and good luck indications.

We explain the use of different remedies each year through our popular *Feng Shui Extravaganzas* which are whole day events held in Singapore, Malaysia, the USA, UK and in 2010, for the first time, also in French Polynesia! These events go a long way towards protecting them against the year's afflictions.

The *Feng Shui Extravaganza* road show is a wonderful way to connect with feng shui enthusiasts and to explain the fine points on what needs to be done each New Year. Those interested to attend any of our 2010 Extravaganzas, the dates and venues can be accessed at www.wofs.com.

Part 5
Improving personal feng shui

Each New Year, in addition to updating your space feng shui, it also benefits to make some spatial adjustments that update your individual feng shui.

The practice of personalised feng shui takes account of your animal sign as well as your individual Kua number. You need to make adjustments to your facing directions and sitting locations to take account of the different energies of the Tiger Year; thus your lucky and unlucky directions as indicated by your Kua number must be fine-tuned to take account of the year's afflictions.

Remember that in using your lucky directions you must always be mindfully aware of the influences of various annual afflictions. Even when a direction is generally considered very "lucky" for you, if in the Year of the Tiger that direction is adversely affected in any way, then you must NOT face that direction. Annual energies usually override Kua number lucky directions. Thus if your love direction is afflicted this year, then it is best not to activate romance luck this year. Personalizing your feng shui makes a big difference, especially in a year as challenging as the Tiger Year 2010. Also, using your birth Lo Shu number to see how it combines with this year's Lo Shu number 8 offers some interesting nuances for you to work with.

Finetuning Your Kua Lucky & Unlucky Directions

The compass based method of using your Kua number to determine if you are East or West group, and also for finding our your lucky and unlucky directions, is one of the easiest ways to practice and benefit from compass formula feng shui. Once you know your lucky directions, all you need to do is to arrange your home and office and the furniture within in a way which enables you to always face at least one of your good luck (and unafflicted) directions. Just doing this will immediately make a difference to your luck for the year.

Lo Shu & Kua Numbers of Sheep People

Birth Year	Element SHEEP	Age in 2010	Lo Shu No. at Birth	KUA No. for Men	KUA No. for Women
1931	Metal Sheep	79	6	6	9
1943	Water Sheep	67	3	3	3
1955	Wood Sheep	55	9	9	6
1967	Fire Sheep	43	6	6	9
1979	Earth Sheep	31	3	3	3
1991	Metal Sheep	19	9	9	6

The formula also identifies 4 different kinds of good luck and 4 severities of bad luck, with each being represented by a compass direction. The 4 good directions allows you to choose whether to face a direction that brings you success, love, good health of improves your personal growth.

The formula also identifies 4 kinds of misfortune directions, describing the nature and intensity of each of these bad luck directions. Once you are aware of your misfortune directions, all you need to do is

PART 5 - IMPROVING PERSONAL FENG SHUI

to systematically change your sitting and sleeping arrangements so that you will never face or have your head pointed to any of the bad luck directions. arrangements so that you will never face or have your head pointed to any of the bad luck directions. Feng shui is really that simple!

But there is one extra thing you need to take account of and that is to finetune these lucky and unlucky directions.

1) Check if any of your **lucky directions** are afflicted by any of the afflictive stars of the New Year. This requires you to study the afflicted directions laid out in the previous chapter.

2) Take note of your own animal sign compass location and ensure it is properly activated and kept free of clutter, even if this is not one of your lucky directions. Remember that your animal sign direction is more important and also overrides the Kua directions!

Your animal sign direction, which in the case of the Sheep is SW1, is always lucky for you irrespective of what the Kua formula indicates. It overrides the Kua formula, but if the direction is afflicted by a bad number star for the year, then the location and direction should be avoided. In the Year of the Tiger, the SW is afflicted by the misfortune star which brings bad luck; so to be on the safe side, it is better for West group Sheep people (those with Kua number 6) to avoid the SW or sleep with head pointed to the SW. Even if SW is lucky for you and brings you the kind of luck you want, it is not advisable to use this direction in 2010. Those of you with Kua numbers 3 and 9 are East group people, so the SW is not a good direction for you anyway, so do take note that the SW is doubly bad for you.

3) You also need to look at your Lo Shu number at birth and see how this interacts with the Lo shu number of the year, which is 8. You should find out whether any of your **lucky directions** are in any way affected by bad luck stars during the year.

Every year, the direction of misfortune bringing afflictions change location so it is vital to make sure that any lucky direction you may be facing – at work or at home which you had previously put into place - is NOT afflicted in 2010.

This is because time sensitive annual afflictions exert greater strength than personalized directions. Indeed, annual energy flow usually possesses greater impact even than Period energies. Time dimension feng

PART 5 - IMPROVING PERSONAL FENG SHUI

Lucky & Unlucky Directions for Sheep

Kua Number	3	6	9
Success Direction	South*	West	East
Love Direction	SE*	SW*	North
Health Direction	North	NE*	SE*
Personal Growth	East	NW	South
Bad Luck Direction	SW*	SE*	NE*
Five Ghosts Direction	NW	East	West
Six Killings Direction	NE*	North	SW*
Total Loss Directions	West	South*	NW

Note: All directions afflicted in 2010 are marked with *. When a direction that is lucky for you is afflicted, you are recommended not to use that direction this year. When the direction afflicted is one of your bad luck directions, then you must extra sure you do not get hurt by facing this direction or occupying this location in your home or office.

shui affects the luck of the world more strongly than the space dimension of feng shui. Only when you practice your feng shui with this particular awareness, will you get the most out of feng shui.

Male and female Sheep born people belong to both East and West group directions as their Kua numbers are 3, 6 and 9 for both men and women. The table on the facing page summarizes the good and bad luck directions for the three Kua numbers 3, 6 and 9.

To Activate Success Luck

Your personalized Success direction is your *sheng chi* direction. If you can face your success direction without being afflicted in any way by the annual afflictions then success luck flows smoothly, bringing advancement, growth and enhanced stature in your professional life. But you MUST make sure your Success direction is not afflicted.

For 2010, all Sheep who belong to Kua 3 have South as their *sheng chi* and this is afflicted by the number 3 star which brings quarrels, courtcases and terrible misunderstandings. For you, it is better to give the South a pass this year and face say East instead, as East has the auspicious energy of heaven luck. Look at your Success direction for those born in the Sheep year summarized in the table and you can

Success Luck for Sheep Born People

Kua Number	3	6	9
Success Direction	South*	West	East

systematically investigate which are the directions that are absolutely taboo for you. Facing either bad luck directions or afflicted directions will have an adverse effect on your success luck.

If you really have no choice and cannot change your facing direction at work even when the direction is afflicted, then first assess whether it is your Success direction that is being hurt and if so, how strong is the affliction. In this case only Sheep with Kua 3 is affected and here the affliction is the number 3 star which can be easily overcome by placing the **Fire Sword** or **Fireball** in front of you.

Kua Number 3

Male and female Sheep with Kua number 3 belong to the East group and for them their *sheng chi* success direction which is South is afflicted by the hostile star 3. This indicates that if you face your Success direction in 2010, your success luck is negatively affected by misunderstandings and arguments which might lead to litigation. This year requires a great deal of patience from you, but the good news is that there is good success luck as indicated in your element horoscope chart. Success luck here indicates that despite the year's feng shui afflictions, you can successfully negotiate your way past obstacles and hindrances.

The presence of good Success luck means that your professional and working life is likely to be smooth during the year and obstacles can be overcome. It will help further if you keep the *wu wang* in your animal sign direction (SW) under control with the **five element bell** or **pagoda**. You should also ensure that arguments that arise through the year do not escalate into big problems.

Remember that the South direction which is your *sheng chi* has this potential to bring are troublesome people into your life, thereby making it difficult to bring your projects to completion. Overcome the number 3 star in the South with the **Flaming Sword**!

Kua Number 6

Male and female Sheep people with Kua number 6 have West as their success direction. You also belong to the West group. This is very auspicious indeed

PART 5 - IMPROVING PERSONAL FENG SHUI

because the West direction brings many good things in 2010.

Mainly, the West direction has two powerfully lucky stars brought by the 24 mountains. These are the stars which are appropriately named Big Auspicious, so facing the West brings this double auspicious benefit for Sheep people with Kua number 6.

Kua Number 9

Those of you Sheep who have 9 as your Kua number belong to the East group and for you, the *sheng chi* Success direction is East, which in 2010 is very auspicious as it is visited by the celestially powerful star of 6. This number brings heaven luck.

The East is flanked by two other empowering stars, the Star of Golden Deity and the Tai Sui, the God of the Year. Thus cosmic energy coming from the East is quite celestial and is extremely powerful and auspicious in 2010. The Chinese always describe superlative luck as coming from the "Gods" or from "heaven" and whenever these indications are listed it means there is potential for good fortune to actualize.

It is a good idea for those of you, male and female, to try and sit facing the East direction to capture the blessings from the celestials. This means the 42 year old Fire Sheep woman and the 54 year old Wood Sheep gentleman. The Wood element of the East also benefits these Sheep people as it strengthens their heavenly stem elements.

To Maintain Good Health

These days, with international travel being so extensive and people around the world on the move so much, there is always the real danger of epidemics spreading across continents. Good health can no longer be taken for granted and it is now advisable not only to keep the energy of the home vibrant and clean, you must also make certain that where you live is always filled with a good supply of yang energy.

It is when chi energy is moving and not stagnating that residents within enjoy good health. A healthy home is where residents enjoy good resistance against bacteria and germs and are not in danger of picking up infectious disease. Thus good health in feng shui terms means you should eat well and auspiciously; and also live well with enough exercise and with no mental stress. When you have a good healthy environment you are unlikely to be vulnerable to illness.

Sickness in any home is almost always due to bad feng shui and also because the house itself is affected by illness star vibrations which are left unchecked, or worst still, which flourish because the environment within fosters it. When someone gets sick in any household, the sickness energy is always infectious so residents will get sick, one by one.

Apart from catching the bug from each other, this is also due to the illness star somehow getting activated; and then it affects everyone irrespective of which part of the house you stay in. Afflictive star influences can move from one part of the house to another if they are not strongly curbed **at source**. This means placing the **metal cures** and the **wu lou** in the **NE** corner which this year is the source of illness vibes.

Health Directions for Sheep Born

Kua Number	3	6	9
Health Direction	North*	NE*	SE*
Bad Luck Direction	SW*	SE*	NE*
6 Killings Direction	NE	North	SW*

For those who want to capture your individual good health direction, you can sleep with the head pointed to your Health direction. This is said to be the direction of the "Heavenly Doctor".

The table on previous page summarizes the good health luck directions for all the Sheep men and women based on their Kua numbers 3, 6 and 9. Note that all the 3 good health luck directions are afflicted in 2010. Those with Kua number 3 have North as their *tien yi* direction and in 2010, North is the place of the Three Killings. Facing North may bring the Doctor from Heaven to you, but for you 67 year old Water Sheep and 31 year old Earth Sheep, please take note that the Three Killings that is located in the North this year can be deadly and perhaps is more than a match for the good doctor from heaven.

Those with Kua 6 have NE as their health direction and this unfortunately is in direct conflict with the feng shui chart of the year. Here it states that the illness star of the year is located exactly where the heavenly doctor is located for Kua 6 people. This affliction definitely makes it impossible for them to face this NE direction. This directly affects the 55 year Wood Sheep Lady as well as the 43 year old Fire Sheep guy.

As for those with Kua 9, your *tien yi* direction is SE and this too is afflicted by the presence of the violent star 7. Thus 79 year old and 43 year old Sheep women should avoid sleeping with their head pointed to the SE as doing so puts you in conflict with the year's violent and robbery star. This definitely does not bring good feng shui. The same advice also applies to the 55 year old Sheep gentleman.

Becoming a Star at School

For the 19 year old Sheep teenager, the year 2010 brings some success luck, so doing well in your exams is definitely a good possibility. But vitality is low and health is not good.

You can harness extra good luck by energizing your Personal Growth direction as this will attract the luck of good concentration for you each time you study, do your homework or revise for school and public examinations. If you can face your Personal Growth direction while studying at home, or when working on an assignment, doing your home work or even when sitting for an examination, it will bring amazing good fortune for you.

The Personal Growth direction for 19 year old female Sheep teenagers is NW (for Kua 6) and for male Sheep teenagers is South (for Kua 9). Of these two directions, note that the South is afflicted by the hostility star 3 and is thus not a lucky direction to capture. Both the East and NW are good directions for 2010 so here the female teenager Sheep can use NW while the male should use East for attracting good attainment luck in 2010.

Attracting Romance

If you are looking for marriage opportunities, you must be careful that you do not meet up with married people pretending to be single. Be extra careful because the *flower of external romance* star is running amok in the Year of the Tiger.

This means the libido of married people, especially married men are at a high. Singles should thus be extra skeptical of new people coming into their lives, especially if they are actively using love rituals to attract romantic opportunities into their lives. Here are three ways to attract love:

1) First you can activate your personalized peach blossom luck. For the Sheep, your peach blossom animal is the Rat. You should place a beautiful, expensive looking Rat in the North location of your bedroom. The Rat is a very special creature in feng shui as it is said to symbolize the wealth-bringing creature used by wealth deities to actualize wealth luck. Do not get any old "Rat" from pavement stalls and flea markets where the energy they are absorbing is unlikely to be very good!

2) Please also note that the Peach Blossom Star lands in the North in 2010. So this powerful love direction will be excellent for activating marriage luck this year.

Nien Yen Direction for Sheep

Kua Number	3	6	9
Love Direction	SE*	SW*	North

For the Sheep, the direction North thus has a double advantage. So, no matter your age, irrespective of whether you have been married before, this is the direction to activate if you want to activate the year's romantic energies.

3) Most effective of all is that you should sleep with your head pointed to your *nien yen* direction. This is shown below for the three Kua numbers that belong to the Sheep, ie 3, 6 and 9. It is the love direction and the best way of making it work for you is to encourage *nien yen* vibrations to enter into your crown chakra while you sleep; but once again do make certain that your *nien yen* direction is not afflicted during the year. The conventional advice to those wanting romance is for you to arrange your beds such that your head points to your *nien yen* direction when you sleep.

Unfortunately for the Sheep interested in romance in 2010, all the three Kua numbers 3, 6 or 9, appear to be afflicted. The SE is hit by the violent 7 while the SW is hit by the Five Yellow and the North has the Three Killings.

Based on this it appears that none of the Sheep this year can successfully use their *nien yen* direction to help them. If you sleep with the head pointing to the SE you could get robbed; to the SW you will attract misfortune luck and if your head is pointed to the North, it could attract the Three Killings into your life. This is a severe affliction and best that you do not run the risk. If you really have to use this direction of North no matter what, then please make certain you are wearing adequate remedy to subdue the star of Three Killings.

Interacting with the Annual Lo Shu Number 8

While the feng shui chart of the year reveals the energy pattern of the year, bringing new energies to every house these also interact with every resident's personal Lo Shu charts. Every animal sign is influenced by three Lo Shu charts which are created using their birth Lo Shu numbers which are not to be confused with the Kua numbers discussed earlier.

The table here reveals the Lo Shu number of those born in the years of the Sheep extracted from the

PART 5 - IMPROVING PERSONAL FENG SHUI

Lo Shu Numbers of Sheep Born People

Birth Year	Element Sheep	Age in 2010	Lo Shu No. at Birth
1931	Metal Sheep	79	6
1943	Water Sheep	67	3
1955	Wood Sheep	55	9
1967	Fire Sheep	43	6
1979	Earth Sheep	31	3
1991	Metal Sheep	19	9

Thousand Year calendar. The Sheep's Lo Shu numbers are 3, 6 or 9 and each is a number from the Lower, Middle and Upper period in the feng shui cycle of three periods which covers 180 years.

The Lo Shu number at birth offers clues to the personality traits of the Sheep and how they interact with the current year's Lo shu number of 8 offer additional nuances to the Sheep's luck outlook for the year.

Sheep with Birth Lo Shu of 6
(affecting the 43 and 79 year old Sheep)

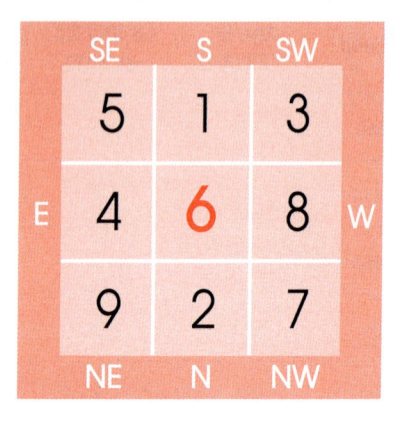

SE	S	SW
5	1	3
4 (E)	6	8 (W)
9	2	7
NE	N	NW

This is the Lo Shu chart for 43 and 79 year old Sheep.

The number 6 is an ally of the number 8, both being white numbers. The number 6 indicates good strength. The element of 6 is Metal, while that of 8 is Earth, so the year tends to exhaust the Sheep whose Lo Shu number is 6. Note also that the SE sector of the Lo Shu chart has the number 5 when the centre number is 6. The two stars 8 and 5 are Earth numbers and Sheep itself is also an Earth sign. This is not necessarily beneficial as there is already a surplus of Earth element in 2010. Also with the 5 in Sheep's direction of SW, this is like a permanent affliction to those of you with Lo Shu 6. You are advised to always wear the **5 element pagoda pendant**.

Sheep with Birth Lo Shu of 3
(affecting the 31 and 67 year old Sheep)

	SE	S	SW	
	2	7	9	
E	1	3	5	W
	6	8	4	
	NE	N	NW	

This is the Lo Shu chart for 31 and 67 year old Sheep.

The Lo Shu number of this Sheep has a Ho Tu combination with the year's number 8, which brings good fortune. Here the Sheep's Lo Shu of 3 is Wood while the year Lo Shu of 8 is Earth, thereby giving greater strength to the Sheep. The Ho Tu combination is very auspicious, definitely bringing success luck. This combination will bring hidden assistance and an energy boost to the Sheep who sorely needs help. Interestingly it is the Water Sheep and the Earth Sheep who have the Lo shu number of 3. As we have seen, Water is the auspicious element of 2010 while Earth stands for wealth in this year's paht chee chart.

Sheep with Birth Lo Shu of 9
(affecting the 19 and 55 year old Sheep)

SE	S	SW
8	4	6
7 (E)	9	2 (W)
3	5	1
NE	N	NW

This is the Lo Shu chart for 19 and 55 year old Sheep.

The number 9 is an auspicious indication which stands for future prosperity luck. The number 9 chart has no direct link with the year's Lo Shu number of 8 other than it follows from 8 thus signifying the immediate future. Sheep people whose Lo Shu number is 9 can build on the year's luck to create something long term.

Note that the number 9 in the centre of the chart causes the celestial number 6 to fly into the Sheep's home location of SW. This is an excellent indication it brings hidden strength and energy to the Sheep. This benefits the 54 year old Wood Sheep.

Safeguarding Sheep's Location in 2010

Use a compass to determine the Sheep direction of your home which is SW1. This refers to the SW sector of the whole house and the SW corner of rooms you frequently use, such as your bedroom or your home office.

You should make sure the toilet, the store room or the kitchen of the house are NOT located in the SW1 direction. If they are it will create a serious feng shui problem for you.

A **toilet** in your Sheep direction flushes away all the luck of residents belonging to the Sheep sign. Career luck is hard hit and recognition will be blocked. Those in business face an array of problems including financial loss. A **store room** here locks up all your good luck. You will find it hard to fly and ambitions will get stalled. A **kitchen** here suppresses all your good luck.

If you envisage staying in the same home for several more years, it is advisable to consider changing the room usage of your SW sector if the toilet or store room are here. When you create an active space where most of your productive work gets done, it energizes your most personally important sector of the home, thereby benefiting you. Always make sure the energy in your animal sign direction is vibrant and active, yang in nature and never has a chance to get stale, because then yin chi starts to accumulate.

The Five Yellow

In 2010, the whole SW sector is afflicted by the Five Yellow also known as the *wu wang* which brings the potential of great misfortune befalling the Sheep. This is basically the affliction that plagues Sheep people throughout the year and it is a good idea to always carry the powerfully effective cure against the 5 star which is **five element pagoda** or **bell**. Metal is also effective against the Five Yellow, which is an Earth star.

Improving your Door Feng Shui

One of the best ways of improving your feng shui in any year is to ensure that the doors you use daily into the house, into your bedroom and into your office are auspicious for you. To determine the best direction to use we always look at the four auspicious directions using the Kua formula of directions.

You can check the tables on the following pages and then use a compass to determine the facing direction that works best for you, and apply them for each of the doors you use most frequently.

PART 5 - IMPROVING PERSONAL FENG SHUI

Auspicious Door Directions for Sheep

Kua Number	9	3	6	9	6	3
Male/Female	Female	Female	Female	Male	Male	Male
Best Door Direction based on Sheng Chi Direction	East	South	West	East	West	South
Best Door Facing Direction in 2010	East	East	West	East	West	East

Be very mindful about the doors you walk under each day. However, making sure the doors bring good luck for you is only the first step in improving your feng shui. It is also important to check if the facing direction of the door is afflicted by the year's energies.

For 2010, all doors that either face, or are located in the SW, NE, South, North and SE are afflicted and will respond positively to antidote remedies.

Here is the list of the correct remedies which you can place either above the door, or flanking it. The more frequently you use the door the more important it is to place these remedies.

Doors referred to also include doors inside the home. These remedies do not send out harmful chi the way the Pa Kua symbol with yin arrangement of trigrams do. In the past, these were the only "cure" known and sold, and many used them indiscriminately, without realizing the potential harm they can cause.

The remedies recommended here can easily correct and subdue afflictions without creating bad chi. This is a very important aspect of cures that we take seriously into consideration. For all **main doors** going into the home, it is an excellent idea also to place the **powerful mantra plaques** done in red and this is because the mantras not only keep all bad vibes out of the house, they also bless everyone who walks under them. This is the best way to practice feng shui – to make sure it benefits you without harming others!

- **For doors facing Southwest,** place the **five element plaque** above the door.
- **For doors facing Northeast,** place the **wu lou door hanging** by the side of the door.
- **For doors facing South,** place the **kalachakra mantra plaque** above the door.
- **For doors facing North,** place the **three celestial guardians** flanking the door.
- **For doors facing Southeast,** place **blue Rhino/Elephant door plaque**.

Rhino & Elephant Door Plaque

Use a good reliable compass to determine your facing direction of all your doors and make sure you stand just in front of the door to determine this. Do note that even when the "door" you use to enter the house is from the garage, and it is only a small side door, it is still very important. In fact the more you use a door the more important it becomes.

Special Enhancers & Amulets for 2010

To ensure stability of luck for your household, it is an excellent idea to activate the center of the home, or at least the center of your living room area with **a crystal globe containing blue coloured water**. We have designed a very special globe in two sizes – a thee inch diameter globe and a six-inch diameter globe that is embossed on the outside with the 12 animal signs of the Zodiac. The globe is an excellent enhancer for the center number of 8 because this is an Earth number.

The Earth element also signifies wealth luck in 2010 so the presence of a crystal globe here is amazingly auspicious. It is beneficial to twirl the globe daily to imbue it with yang energy. The water inside symbolically brings much needed water element into the living area. This is because the paht chee chart tells us that Water is terribly lacking in 2010. Note that to Taoist masters even "a single drop of water can represent an entire ocean". Hence water enhancers are so good for 2010!

For the Sheep person, it is an excellent idea to place a Sheep/goat image next to the globe, letting it face SW. This creates good energy for your particular animal sign and should you so wish, you can also place your secret friend the Horse, as well as your allies, the Rabbit and Boar images here as well. This will create excellent friendship energy bringing harmony and balance into your life. Special note for Sheep - please note that your secret friend the Horse enjoys excellent chi energy this year, so stick close to your Horse friends in 2010!

PART 5 - IMPROVING PERSONAL FENG SHUI

Special Talismans for the Sheep

In 2010, the Sheep person benefits from the following cures and talismans:

- Invite a **Golden Deity** into your home to help bring you some success luck. This can be any of the deities that appeal to you. Look for the **Dzambhala that sits on a Dragon** as this will also bring you wealth luck.

- The **Namgylma Stupa** to protect against misfortunes and fatal accidents. Namgylma is the powerful Goddess of Longevity with 3 faces. She is also known as Ushnisha Vijaya. Her image and mantras that surround the stupa protect against premature death and natural disasters. She also brings wonderful new meaning into your life, surrounding you with an aura of great happiness. Displaying her Stupa in your home brings protection as well as happiness and contentment.

Namgylma Stupa

- The **Blue Rhino and Elephant** to guard against robbery and break-ins. Display near the main entrance of your home or in the SE, the place of the burglary star this year. You should also be more careful in March 2010 and January 2011. This is when the burglary star enters your home direction. In these months, it is best to also carry a blue rhino and elephant charm or hanging with you whenever you are out and about.

- Get a **Fan with Om Mani mantra** to ward of infidelity dangers in your marriage. Ladies keep this inside your bag and use it as often as you can. The star of external romance is prominent in this Tiger Year, so those of you who are married should not take chances.

Fan with Om Mani Mantra

PART 5 - IMPROVING PERSONAL FENG SHUI   223

The 24 Mountains in 2010

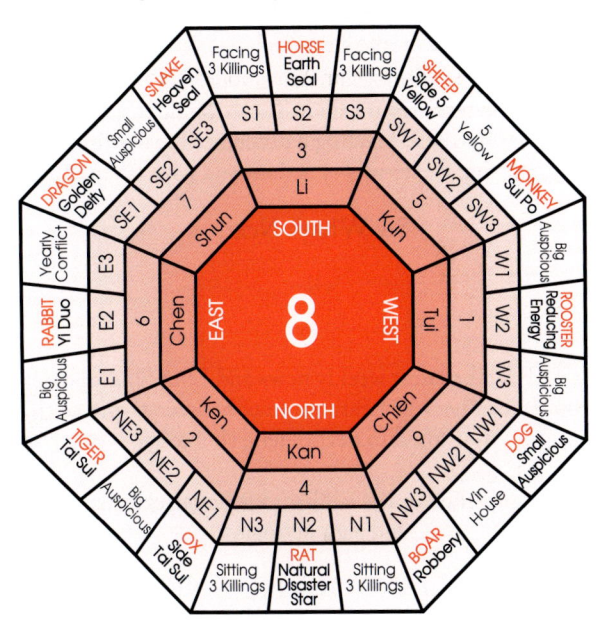

The number 8 dominates the year 2010 bringing auspicious energy to the Tiger Year. The 12 animals signs play host to the stars of the 24 mountains. These indicate the kind of cosmic forces influencing the luck for the year.

WANT TO LEARN MORE?

Don't Stop Now!

We hope you enjoyed reading your own personal horoscope book from Lillian Too & Jennifer Too. You are probably already feeling a difference in your life and enjoying the results of actions you have taken!

So, What's Next?

LILLIAN TOO'S FREE
Online Weekly Ezine NEW!

It's FREE! The latest weekly news and Feng Shui updates from Lillian herself! Learn more of her secrets and open your mind to deeper feng shui today.

Just go online to www.lilliantoomandalaezine.com and sign up today!

LILLIAN TOO's FREE NEW
Online Weekly Ezine!

Don't Miss Out! Join thousands of others who are already receiving their **FREE** updates delivered to their inbox each week.

Lillian's NEW Online FREE Weekly Ezine is only available to those who register online at www.lilliantoomandalaezine.com